Gardening
for
Mindfulness

An Hachette UK Company
www.hachette.co.uk

First published in Great Britain in 2017
by Mitchell Beazley
an imprint of Octopus Publishing Group
Carmelite House
50 Victoria Embankment
London EC4Y 0DZ
www.octopusbooks.co.uk
www.octopusbooksusa.com

Published in association with The Royal
Horticultural Society

This edition published in 2020

Distributed in the US by
Hachette Book Group
1290 Avenue of the Americas
4th and 5th Floors
New York, NY 10104

Distributed in Canada by
Canadian Manda Group
664 Annette St.
Toronto, Ontario, Canada M6S 2C8

ISBN 978-1-78472-661-4

A CIP catalogue record for this book is
available from the British Library.

Printed and bound in China

10 9 8 7 6 5 4 3 2 1

Publisher: Alison Starling
Editor: Pollyanna Poulter
Art Director: Juliette Norsworthy
Designer: Rosamund Saunders
Picture Research Manager:
Giulia Hetherington
Senior Production Controller:
Allison Gonsalves
RHS Publisher: Rae Spencer-Jones
RHS Editor: Simon Maughan

Gardening
for
Mindfulness

HOLLY FARRELL

CONTENTS

How to use this book

There is guidance and inspiration here for the practised and the novice at both gardening and mindfulness.

The first chapter, *What is mindfulness?*, describes the concept and background of mindfulness and includes an introductory exercise: studying a flower in all its beauty. The benefits of incorporating mindfulness and gardening into your life are also explained. The next chapter, *Mindfulness and gardening*, outlines the compatibility and benefits of gardening and mindfulness practice. It then details the basic principles of mindfulness and how to get started, where to practise meditation in the garden and how to set about taking a mindful walk.

A mindful garden suggests design tricks and plants to enhance the possibilities for mindful gardening – those plants that especially stimulate each of the five senses are listed, including suggestions for balcony and indoor gardens. The next two chapters go into more detail about how to apply mindfulness to everyday gardening tasks. *Mindful garden practice* is more relevant to readers already gardening, and covers the main jobs for each season in turn and how to do them in a more mindful manner. *Mindful garden projects* are more for the novice gardener, though equally applicable to the more experienced: this chapter offers self-contained small schemes such as creating a mandala and planting a herb garden, with specific growing instructions as well as mindful guidance.

A *Shed reminder sheet* summarizes the teachings, giving a few pointers to remember. It is designed to be stuck up somewhere you will see it before heading out into the garden. Finally, *Further resources* gives some suggestions of where to go for more information on both gardening and mindfulness.

Yes, I remember Adlestrop –
The name, because one afternoon
Of heat the express-train drew up there
Unwontedly. It was late June.

The steam hissed. Someone cleared his throat.
No one left and no one came
On the bare platform. What I saw
Was Adlestrop – only the name

And willows, willow-herb, and grass,
And meadowsweet, and haycocks dry,
No whit less still and lonely fair
Than the high cloudlets in the sky.

And for that minute a blackbird sang
Close by, and round him, mistier,
Farther and farther, all the birds
Of Oxfordshire and Gloucestershire.

Edward Thomas,

ADLESTROP

CHAPTER 1

What is mindfulness?

The 1914 poem *Adlestrop* (see page 7) is a perfect example of mindfulness. Imagine the more likely scenario today: the train stops at the station, but who is paying attention? How many of us would be looking not out of the window but at a phone screen, a laptop, or both? We would probably be blocking out the world with headphones as well, and worrying about a meeting that we had earlier in the day or work we still have to do tomorrow. When we get home we do not really remember the journey itself, though we might have registered the annoying fact that the train stopped when it should not have and made us late. How much more pleasant would the trip have been if we had looked out of the window and really seen and heard what was happening around us? We are so busy planning for the future and dwelling on the past that we are forgetting to live in the present. Life is passing us by.

Mindfulness is the solution to this problem. Through exercising the brain, we can teach ourselves to pay attention. It is not by chanting or meditation; it is not a religion, theory or belief; it is simply learning to focus, and such a beneficial practice is supported by many neuroscientists. Mindfulness is a simple concept and easy to learn. We do not even have to set aside dedicated time to become mindful: we can incorporate it into our daily lives, and what better place than in the garden?

Put simply, mindfulness is paying attention. So many of our actions are habitual, and there are so many distractions in modern life, that it is all too easy to adopt autopilot. Conversations with friends or family are only half-listened to because we are thinking about the many things we need to do next, and meals are only half-tasted as we are busy watching a screen.

Mindfulness can also help us deal with unpleasant or negative emotions such as anxiety, stress, grief and depression. In mindfulness practice the aim is not to change feelings or sweep them under the carpet, but rather to accept that this is how we are; there is no reason to berate ourselves for not being "better". By letting these thoughts come and go, observing them but not getting caught up in them, we can create some distance and realize that the feelings do not define us and that they will not last forever. Think of thoughts as cars on a busy road: being stuck in the middle of that road, dodging the traffic in a panicked and terrifying attempt to stay alive, is the material of nightmares. Far better to sit at the side of the road and just watch the cars go by. We learn how to observe rather than feel these thoughts by continually bringing the focus back to our senses whenever we become distracted.

That is all there is to it. Mindfulness is simply being aware and in a state of alert attention that allows the mind to go quiet. It is purely and simply living in the moment and experiencing it fully – being present. Thoughts and distractions are not pushed away or buried. Instead they are allowed to arise and then the attention is brought back entirely to the senses and the task in hand, giving the mind a rest from the constant chatter and worries and allowing you time to get on with enjoying life. Noticing we have become distracted by our thoughts is in itself being mindful. Meditation is a tool, an exercise, that can be used to practise mindfulness, but it does not define it.

How to practice mindfulness

There are two basic ways to practise mindfulness. The first is to sit in silence and focus the mind on your breath as it moves in and out of your body (a meditative exercise). Every time you realize that your mind has wandered away from the exercise, distracted perhaps by a noise or thought, your attention is brought back to your breath.

The other method works in exactly the same way except that the practice is active and incorporated into an everyday task. While performing habitual actions, such as mowing the lawn, you tether your attention to a particular sense: for example, the feeling as you walk up and down on the grass.

The benefits of mindfulness and gardening

It may seem counterintuitive to take time out to contemplate life, but if we do not we are more liable to waste it. Battling on, without really noticing anything else, becomes a mindset and a detrimental one at that. It is how we can sit at a desk for hours, manfully trying to finish a piece of work, and not notice until we finish just how very tired, hungry, cold and stiff we are. Chopping logs with a blunt axe, and thinking there is no time to stop and sharpen it, is a slow and painful business. By taking a break to sharpen the axe, and refuel, we can go back to the task feeling stronger and do it faster and better – and finish sooner. Mindfulness allows us to sit down mentally for a moment, and gives both the mind and body a break.

Adopting autopilot can help us to get through the day, but we lose so many opportunities to enjoy life that way. By introducing mindfulness to our lives, we can truly engage with our friends and family, truly taste that amazing meal that we have saved up for, truly see the sights on our once-in-a-lifetime holiday. When we experience them fully, with our senses rather than our thoughts, we also remember them more clearly.

> "One of the most tragic things I know about human nature is that all of us tend to put off living. We are all dreaming about some magical rose garden over the horizon instead of enjoying the roses blooming under our window."

Rosa 'Paul's Himalayan Musk' (rose)

Dale Carnegie,
WRITER

DIMINISHING THE EFFECTS OF NEGATIVE EMOTIONS

Mindfulness can also teach us how to turn down the volume of our internal critic. It is all too easy for worries and negative emotions to spiral out of control, but by observing our thoughts as they come and go, without judgment, we learn that we are not our thoughts. It is all too easy to seek refuge from painful feelings in external distractions – comfort eating, retail therapy, alcohol – without ever addressing the root cause. Looking at these emotions candidly can be difficult, but mindfulness teaches us to view our faults with kindness: in other words, not to criticize ourselves for having self-critical thoughts, not to worry about being worried, or to get stressed about being stressed. We can break the cycle, change the way we relate to our negative emotions, and therefore reduce their effects. This also helps to declutter the mind, so that when we do think about something we can focus on it entirely, more productively and creatively.

MINDFULNESS AS MEDICINE

The positive effects of mindfulness on a range of stress-related illnesses have resulted in it being approved by major national health services in some countries across the world in the form of mindfulness based-cognitive therapy. Numerous studies have shown its benefits in managing illnesses such as depression and in reducing incidences of stress and anxiety. Mindfulness based-cognitive therapy has also been shown to improve focus, creativity and relationships.

REAPING THE BENEFITS

Gardening and being outdoors also have many proven benefits, not just to the body but also to the mind. Of course, this is by no means news – the Victorians had farms in the grounds of their mental health institutions in which the patients could work, while the benefits of gardening for the mentally ill was documented in the US as far back as 1798 – but what many gardeners have always known is now being backed up by hard evidence from clinical studies. A report into the health and wellbeing benefits of allotment gardening found that the gardeners had better self-esteem and general health, as well as lower levels of depression and fatigue, than the non-gardeners. The Ecominds projects run by the UK mental health charity Mind gave 12,000 people with mental health problems the opportunity to get active outdoors; 70 per cent of these people experienced significant increases in mental wellbeing by the time they had finished their project. The American Horticultural Therapy Association (AHTA) was formed in 1973, and now oversees the provision of gardening therapy in a wide range of settings, while in the UK the National Health Service (NHS) is also now starting to pilot prescribing gardening, as well as mindfulness, as a means of making people feel better. Across the world, there is a growing awareness that mental health problems carry a huge social and economic cost, and that medicine (pills) can treat only a small percentage of the problem. Social prescribing, as it is called, addresses the rest of the patient's life.

Gardening, like mindfulness, is a way of finding a sense of calm in an otherwise chaotic world. It offers a simpler existence, an antidote to the generally sedentary and virtual lives we lead, even if it is practised for only a few minutes. Both gardening and mindfulness forge a connection to the world around us – to nature, wildlife and people – which can bring pleasure and peace. Working the soil is so ingrained in our evolution and psyche that even those who have never gardened can find familiarity and comfort in tending to plants and the earth. The physical exercise releases endorphins (happy chemicals) in our brain. Social interaction – with fellow allotment holders and neighbours over the garden fence or through garden clubs – and giving away produce and plants to friends and family all promote good mental health. The New Economics Foundation has defined five evidence-based ways to mental wellbeing: connection with others; being more active; keeping learning; giving to others; and taking notice of the world. Gardening fulfils all five of these criteria, with ease.

Mindfulness: some background

MINDFULNESS AND SPIRITUALITY

Although there is no need or obligation to include any religion in our
learning to be mindful, mindfulness has many of its origins in the meditations
of Buddhist monks. These monks use silent contemplation as one means of
achieving enlightenment, and the practical aspects of that meditation – that
is, how actually to do it – are very similar to mindfulness exercises.

The Buddhists' philosophical meditations may seem a world apart from
down-to-earth practical gardening, but the religion has a strong link with the
natural world, and many of its teachings are practical and applicable even if
you do not subscribe to the whole religion. Buddhists use the symbol of the
lotus (*Nelumbo*) flower to illustrate that, even in a muddy swamp, there can
be pure unblemished beauty, and they also adopt the metaphor of the sky to
explain the mind. The true nature of the mind is pure. From time to time,
or perhaps all the time, it can be obscured by clouds of negative emotions
and thoughts, but the sky is not the clouds. The sky is still there *behind* the
clouds, blue, pure and free, and all we have to do is clear the clouds away.

It is all too easy to ascribe our feelings to external causes. Mankind is in
perpetual pursuit of happiness, yet at our advanced stage of civilization
why have we yet to achieve it? We seem to be lonelier, more anxious and
unhappier than ever. The answer, of course, is that money cannot buy us
happiness. Studies of lottery winners have proved that. Once our basic needs
are accounted for – a roof over our heads, food in our bellies – everything else
just becomes so much nonsense. The more we acquire, the less satisfied we
are. Our old car, house or spouse were not intrinsically boring – we were just
bored with them.

Gerbera
(Transvaal daisies)

It may seem to be stating the obvious, but our mind is central to our experience of life. Three people dropped at the starting line of a marathon could have three different attitudes: one might want to run, seeing the challenge; one might be scared of the potential for injury or embarrassment; and one just might not see the point of running where there is no actual need to. Their attitudes are framed purely and solely by their own minds, a product of past experiences and behaviour reinforced by repetition and habit over the years. If we have a tendency to be grumpy, we will be grumpy. We can blame the grumpiness on a bad day at work, the bus being late or on not having enough lunch, but the fact is that we will always find something to be grumpy about, and seek someone else to blame for it.

Buddhism teaches that we need to look not outside but inside, so that we can start to seek contentment and enlightenment by taking action to address the root causes of our unhapiness or problems. We can avoid blaming others for our own discontent, and potentially avoid vast expense trying to buy our way to happiness. Mindful meditation helps us to see the more troubling aspects of our minds without apology or condemnation, and to forge new ways of thinking by simply focusing on the present.

MODERN NEUROSCIENCE

"Neurons that fire together, wire together" is the mantra of the neuroscientists. Our brains are far from fixed organs, because they are evolving and changing all the time; this trait is known as neuroplasticity. Thus the brain is always mouldable and can be taught new skills – it just takes time, patience and practice. Old, negative, destructive patterns of thinking exist because they are routes often travelled in the mind and are thus short cuts. For example, if we take a short cut over the lawn to the shed rather than using the path, a line will be worn in the grass. When the same short cut over the lawn is taken over many years, the main path may have become so overgrown that it is impossible to find. However, the great strength of neuroplasticity is also its fatal weakness: because the brain is plastic we do not *have* to follow the short cut across the lawn. Instead we can choose to go along the path, and the more times we do this, the more the grass grows back over the short cut and eventually returns to pristine lawn. Meanwhile the path has become the default route.

Thus all actions we take make an imprint on our mind. The more often we do something, the more often those neurons fire together and the stronger the wiring between them.

Many neuroscientists would argue that it is more interesting and more relevant to our everyday lives to be able to map and understand the brain, in the way that we already do our bodies, than it is to learn about outer space. What we already know is that the evolution of the human brain has not been as advanced in some areas as others. There are two systems that run parallel in the brain: the sympathetic and parasympathetic nervous systems.

The former is our default position, and unfortunately it is the one that controls our response to emergencies – our fight/flight/freeze button. The sympathetic nervous system also distributes hormones such as adrenaline and cortisol (the stress hormone) through our bodies and, because of a glitch in our programming, all too often can get stuck in a feedback loop whereby we unconsciously believe we are in a state of constant emergency, while consciously we are getting stressed about being stressed. Long-term exposure to cortisol in this way increases the heart rate and blood pressure, and suppresses the digestive and reproductive systems (in a fight or flight situation, these are low priorities). It also weakens the brain, especially in the areas of memory, which is why we cannot remember anything when we are stressed. Perhaps most importantly cortisol suppresses the immune system, making us not only more susceptible to minor infections such as colds and flu, but also predisposing us toward a raft of major illnesses from heart disease, diabetes and obesity to mental disorders and dementia.

The parasympathetic nervous system is the one that signals to the brain that it can relax, that something was a false alarm and that there is nothing to be scared of. Heart rate and blood pressure are lower and the body's energy is rerouted back into the brain and other major organs, as it should be. Obviously this is a preferable place to be, but, because we are unconsciously still always looking out for a predator or other source of trouble, our brain defaults to panic mode and, being stressed, we default to autopilot just to get through the day. We need to work at regulating our brains and steering them more toward the parasympathetic than the sympathetic nervous system. This is possible through mindfulness, because by noticing what is happening in our minds we can train them to know that the possibility of a sabre-toothed tiger in the office is pretty unlikely.

This wild flower meadow includes poppies (*Papaver rhoeas*), ox-eye daisies (*Leucanthemum vulgare*) and cornflowers (*Centaurea cyanus*)

Practice and persistence

By taking time in our day to practise mindfulness we are able to rehearse coming off autopilot and not getting caught up in our thoughts. The more we do so, the easier it becomes, and we can fully experience life rather than letting it pass by while we think about something else. The aim is not to change the mind. The mind, after only a few short attempts at mindfulness, will start to change itself (this has been shown by neuroscientists performing brain scans on people before, after and even during mindfulness practice). In this, and in most other aspects of mindfulness, it can therefore be seen that both the Buddhist and the scientific approaches are much the same.

It takes only a few minutes of mindful practice every day to start rerouting our brains, but even finding time to do this as meditation can be difficult for many people. The answer therefore is to incorporate the mindfulness practice into everyday life, and the garden is an ideal location for this. The focus on the breath is replaced with one on the task at hand and the experience of the senses. Every time the attention wanders, there is a sight, smell, sound, touch or taste in the garden to bring the mind back to the here and now. Unfortunately, it is the brain's natural state to be easily distracted (always checking around for that predator), so it takes time and effort to teach it to focus, especially in the face of modern technology, which feeds that distraction all too easily. However, the more often we notice that our mind has wandered, and bring the focus back onto the senses or breath, the stronger that muscle in our brain gets. For the brain is a muscle, and it needs a regular workout to keep it in shape. As Hercule Poirot would have it, we must "exercise ze leetle grey cells".

Mindfulness is an easy fix for many of our problems, but it is not a quick fix. Like creating a beautiful garden from a muddy field, it takes time and persistence. If, in that garden, we water the weeds and not the flowers, it is the weeds that will grow. The same is true of our positive and negative actions and thoughts: the more we cultivate the negativity, the faster and stronger it will grow. Strengthening the mind helps us cope better with whatever life throws our way.

All too often it takes a near-miss accident, terminal diagnosis or other horrible life event to prompt us to realize that we want to live our lives differently. Mindfulness is not necessarily going to make you want to change your life, but it will enable you to experience it to the full. Some proponents of mindfulness suggest that as a race we are careering toward mental disaster. Whether or not you believe that to be true, there is no time like the present. Do not think that you will start living once you get to the end of your to-do list; instead start incorporating mindfulness into your daily routine now and notice the difference it makes.

The study of a flower

Use this exercise as an initial introduction to mindfulness, and as a restful contemplation whenever you feel you need it.

Start by choosing a flower: it could be any flower you particularly like, or else one that you happen to have around. Ideally the flower would still be on the plant in the garden, but a cut flower is just as effective here. The flower need not be the finest example in the garden – the point of the exercise is to bring your attention solely onto the flower and really notice it in all its glory, whatever it looks like.

Find somewhere to sit – perhaps a shady spot in the garden, at the kitchen table or on the floor – and make yourself comfortable. Ensure you will not be interrupted; leave your phone in another room and turn off the radio and TV if appropriate. Read through the rest of the exercise below and then put the book to one side as you contemplate the flower. You do not need to refer back to it to make sure you are doing it right; the sole purpose is to spend a little time looking properly at the flower, keeping the focus on what you are experiencing.

The suggested things to look for are pointers only and use the sense of sight as the main anchor for the mind. However, if there are other senses stimulated by the study – the sound of insects buzzing in the flower, for example, or if you want to brush the petals to feel their texture – it is perfectly fine to focus on those too.

Take as long as you like to do this exercise, but try and make it at least five minutes. If at any point you realize you have become distracted – your thoughts have wandered off – do not berate yourself for it; it is an entirely natural instinct of the brain. Gently bring the focus back to the flower through the sensory anchors and continue. By the time you have reached a natural conclusion, you will feel that you have actually seen the flower, something that you may never have done before.

The actual exercise

 Take a few deep breaths – in through the nose and out through the mouth – and feel your body relax with each out-breath. Notice where your body is touching the chair or floor, and where the weight of your body is pressing down on those points. Shift your position if you have just noticed any discomfort. Continue with a few more deep breaths, this time concentrating on the chest or stomach as it rises and falls.

 Then bring your attention to the flower. What do you see? Try to avoid describing it to yourself – just look at it. In other words, you do not want to be narrating what you are doing to yourself ("I am looking at the rose and it is red").

 What colour are the petals? Now look more closely – how does the colour change between the internal and external petals, the base and tip of the petals? See the nuances. How do light and shade play across the flower? Are the petals moving in the breeze? Are there drops of rain or dew still beaded there? Does the texture look smooth or velvety? Are the petals thin or thick?

 What about the centre of the flower? Is it domed or flat, or are the pollen-bearing anthers and the stigma (which receives the pollen) held high in isolation? Can you see the pollen? Has the flower just opened or has it been pollinated already – are the petals looking as if they will fall soon? Are there any insects on the flower? If so, watch them going about their business, observing how they move.

 Does the stem hold the flower upright, or is it nodding – or drooping even? Has the plant turned the flower toward the sun? Is the stem smooth or hairy? What shade of green or brown is it, and does that change along its length? Can you see more flower buds or leaves emerging from the stem?

 Then look at the green parts of the flower, that is the calyx/sepals from which the flower bud originally emerged. Are they still green, or fading and browning now? Are there leaves held close behind the flower? What shade are they? What shape? Are the leaf edges smooth or serrated?

 Finally, take a deep breath with your nose close to the flower, inhaling the fragrance (be it floral and sweet or fresh and grassy).

"Flowers are restful to look at. They
have neither emotions nor conflicts."

Sigmund Freud,
PSYCHOANALYST

CHAPTER 2
Mindfulness and gardening

What is a garden?

The garden as a place for leisure is a relatively modern concept. Early gardens were little more than small domestic farms – places to grow food and medicines. It was not until the 16th century that flower gardens, created solely for their beauty rather than their usefulness, were designed. Initially, as with most fashions, it was only the rich who could afford to dedicate a space in the garden purely to pleasure – for the poor, the lavender bush was only a good place to dry the laundry. Gradually, however, the middle classes, then the working classes, were able to turn over more space to growing flowers, trees and shrubs, just because they wanted to. Indeed, private gardens were places in which people could exercise more control than they were able to in the rest of their lives:

"The garden was an escape, a source of renewed vitality, a private domain which the gardener, however beaten down by the world, could order, arrange and manipulate without fear of contradiction."

Keith Thomas,
MAN AND THE NATURAL WORLD

These days we have fewer reasons to use the garden as a place to be "lord of all, the sole despotic governor of every living thing" (John Laurence, 1716), and less need for it to supply our food – so what is a garden? The *Oxford English Dictionary* defines a garden as "a piece of ground, usually partly grassed and adjoining a private house, used for growing flowers, fruit or vegetables, and as a place of recreation", and goes on to note that garden plants are "cultivated, not wild".

To create a garden is to accept that gardening is interfering with plants and how they might want to grow. The mindful gardener does this with care and attention, and an understanding of each plant's needs, so that any and all interference can be purposeful and effective, not just for the gardener but for each plant as well. It is also worth bearing in mind that, by creating gardens, we dramatically increase the diversity of flora and fauna in any given place, so we are actually improving on what Nature would have put there itself.

Each individual component of a garden does not define the garden either, but to say that a garden is merely some combination of lawn and a few flower beds (as the *Oxford English Dictionary* does) is to do it a disservice. A garden is more than the sum of its parts, but it defies definition too, because it is constantly changing, growing, evolving. Moreover our attitude toward it is also constantly in flux. Each garden is unique and reflects our personality, both in its appearance and in what it means to us. Each gardener will feel differently about his or her own garden. For some, gardening will hark back to childhood pleasures of making mud pies and playing with sand, while to others plants are a palette with which to paint a masterpiece.

A "garden" is therefore merely a label – just as "rainbow" is a label – and its true meaning depends on many factors, not least of which is the position of the observer. Thus, although a garden is literally grounded in the mud and plants, it is at the same time fleeting and even illusory. How we look at our garden creates our garden, and so our state of mind affects our gardening.

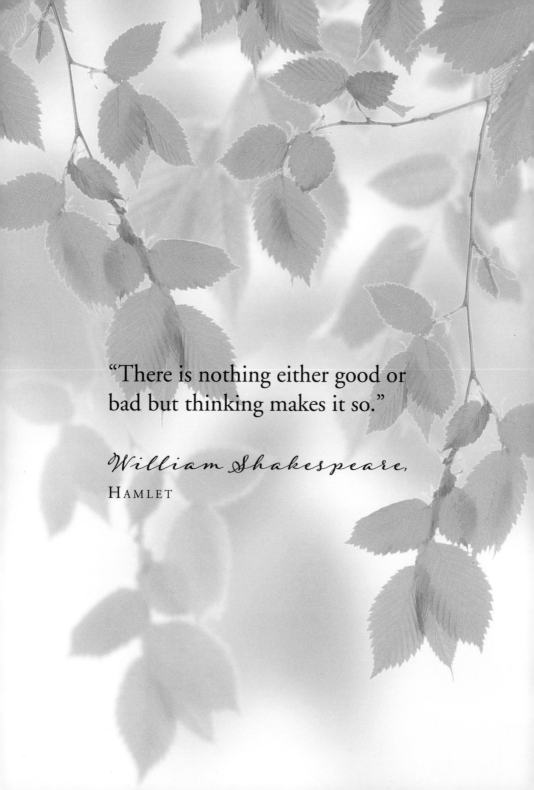

"There is nothing either good or
bad but thinking makes it so."

William Shakespeare,
HAMLET

Natural metaphors

Ground yourself. Blooming. Coming to fruition. Going to seed. We use gardening and natural metaphors to describe our personal and professional lives without thinking about it. We give flowers when words are not enough. Gardens and plants so suffuse mankind's collective psyche that even those who do not particularly enjoy being "in" Nature can appreciate its value and understand the language of plants.

The use of the natural world to provide metaphors and similes to describe and explain is particularly apparent in the teachings of mindfulness. In part this is due to the Buddhist origins of many mindfulness teachers and it is partly because Nature is such a universal language, showing again how suitable gardening is for the practice of mindfulness.

First and foremost we must care for ourselves, as we do our plants. We require space and light to grow, to be fed and watered well. We must look after the soil – our surroundings – so that we can flourish. We need time to rest as well, as plants do every year. If we tended to our bodies and minds as we do our gardens (be it a large estate or a single pot plant), we would be making a very good start indeed.

Buddhist literature also compares negative thoughts and emotions to weeds, and positive feelings to flowers. Whichever gets the most attention – water, space to grow – will flourish, potentially smothering the other. Obviously it is preferable that the flowers do better than the weeds. When we consider our intended plantings, some do well, others fail. Looking back at the border – at our life – which plants have taken over, which have been shaded out? Is the effect what we intended?

A vibrant collection of zinnias

Another way of looking at mindfulness is to consider cause and effect: if we sow a bean seed, a bean plant will grow. All our actions have results, and even small actions can have massive consequences (what if we had sown an acorn?). If we do not plant the bean seed, we will not get the bean plant, but similarly, if we choose to plant a weed seed, then we will get a weed. The neuroscience is in agreement here: all our actions and thoughts cause neurons to fire together. Negative actions and thoughts reinforce the negative wiring, while positive actions and thoughts strengthen the positive wiring.

The acknowledgment that our emotions do not last forever is a central branch of the practice of mindfulness, and it can also help us to come to terms with loss, especially in a garden setting. Plants die, yes, but by making them into garden compost they give life to the next generation of growth and we learn to see the compost in the flower as well as the flower in the compost. For other plants, such as apples or wheat, the flower must die in order that the fruit and its seed may grow. Mourning the flower ignores the potential of the next stage of life; nothing is permanent.

The garden is an excellent place to appreciate the interconnectedness of Nature. Some believe in a life force, an energy that seeps through all living things, but there are cycles and links in a purely scientific outlook as well. The sweat beading on our brows as we dig evaporates, joining the clouds that rain water down on our plants. Light and dark are tropes for good and evil, or ignorance and enlightenment, in all languages, yet consider how a plant actually grows. It absorbs sunlight during the day, but it is at night that most of its growth actually occurs. The plant needs the dark as much as the light; the two are not opposite but linked. Appreciating the interconnections allows us to develop empathy, which helps take the focus away from the "me, me, me" of our own minds and their thoughts.

Nurturing nature

"A garden is a grand teacher. It teaches patience and careful watchfulness; it teaches industry and thrift; above all it teaches entire trust."

Gertrude Jekyll,
GARDEN DESIGNER AND AUTHOR

We entrust ourselves to Nature in a garden, just as much as it entrusts itself to us. We do the best we can to look after the soil, plants and wildlife, and in return Nature brings rain and sunshine so that our seeds – sown in an act of faith – germinate and our plants bear flowers and fruit. However, as anyone knows who has carefully tended a row of lettuce seedlings only to have them ravaged by slugs, or who has lost a prized tree to a storm, Nature can also be cruel and aggressive, and the gardener does not tend to excessively romanticize it.

The lesson we can learn from this is that we cannot control everything, and that it is unwise to try. Furthermore Nature will do things in its own time – snowdrops (*Galanthus*) will emerge and bloom when they are ready, not before, no matter how anxious we are to see them. Attempting to force change on the natural order of things is possible (for example, forced hyacinths for early winter or courgettes/zucchini sown outside in late winter), but is it desirable? "To every thing, there is a season" (Ecclesiastes 3:1). When we garden, we need patience. Because we cannot jump to the end-result, we are naturally steered toward being aware, being present in the process of gardening.

If there is one thing that everyone agrees on, whether of a scientific or religious bent, it is that Nature is literally incredible. The more we discover about its intricacies and workings, the more amazing it becomes. To some this is evidence of an all-powerful creator, while to others it is proof of the complexities of evolution, but everyone can acknowledge the wonder of it all. Plants are not sentient beings; they do not appreciate the finer points of William Shakespeare, Giacomo Puccini's *Tosca* or John Constable's *The Hay Wain*, so it is tempting to think of them as lesser organisms. But consider how plants are able to respond to minute changes in temperature, day length and light direction, which we cannot detect without the aid of technical equipment. Perhaps they are not so dumb after all. Add to that the unique ability of plants to make their own food, and we have a very sophisticated organism indeed, something worth being mindful of as we work through the borders or tend to our pots.

It is natural to want to strive for perfection in many aspects – all aspects perhaps – of our lives, the garden being one. Perfection in a natural setting is completely achievable, but (and here is the rub) it depends on one's definition of perfection. Gardens are in perpetual flux, and so while we may be able to get a garden looking absolutely perfect one day, it will have changed by the following morning. Likewise gardens do not care if we are going on holiday; there will always be setbacks and challenges. However, if we accept that perfection – like all other states and emotions – is impermanent, we can regularly reach that goal.

From a mindfulness perspective, the biggest lesson Nature can teach us is to just be. Nature does not complain, get caught up in its own thoughts or wish for a different life; it just gets on with doing what it is doing. Even the showiest blooms are just being flowers, without vanity or apology. Fruit does not care whether it is eaten by us or by the birds and worms. Many of the inevitable mugs or tea towels that gardeners receive as gifts are inscribed with

Sunflowers *(Helianthus annuus)*

"I'd rather be in the garden", but it is crucial not to think in this way. Even if stuck at the office or in a traffic jam, the point of mindfulness is to be present where we are right now, not daydreaming and wishing we were somewhere else. Although where we are at that moment might not be especially enjoyable, only by fully experiencing the boredom can we better appreciate the more interesting, more fun parts of life.

This is not to say that we should feel powerless, or unable to change anything, for of course being able to improve our situation is one of the great advantages we have as a self-determining species, but the point of mindfulness is to be not always wishing things were better, or different. Rather we learn to greater appreciate what we have, and perhaps realize that we are pretty happy where we are after all. Plants do not daydream, or think "If only I had purple flowers instead of red ones, then I could be happy"; they simply get on with their allotted life and do the best they can with what they have. The idiom that we do not miss the water until the well runs dry has been rerun many, many times in all manner of cultural forms, signifying how little we heed the advice. But if change does need to be made, the greater focus and clarity that mindfulness gives enables us to make those changes with a positive direction and full understanding that it is what is needed.

It is humbling to look Nature full in the face and realize the wealth of its knowledge and power, but it is also just as nurturing of us as we are of it. For a start it lets us learn from its mistakes – and it has more than four billion years' worth of experience – and mindful gardeners are wise to align Nature's interests with their own as far as possible. Beyond that, though, many people feel comforted, appeased or simply at home in a garden. Whether or not you believe in an all-encompassing life force, or any particular religion, it is encouraging to know that, although Nature may have its own ideas about how things are run, we have a place in those plans. It is called Mother Nature after all.

Becoming a better gardener

Mindful gardeners notice more. When we really look at the garden, giving it our full attention, we see all the plants, not just the flowering or big ones. That dogwood (*Cornus*), so obvious with its colourful bare stems in winter, might blend into the background in summer, but its delicate leaves contrast so prettily with the stems if you take the trouble to look. The very small plants at our feet at the front of the border might be overlooked, literally, but if we are mindful we will see them in all their delicate, miniature beauty too, and not just as low-growing space fillers.

Mindful gardening helps us to notice the changes in plants as well – a new leaf here, the first flower to open, the setting of fruit. Carrying this awareness into the kitchen with our home-grown produce can also bring mindfulness to mealtimes. We are much more likely to pay attention to what we are eating when we have put time and effort into growing it ourselves, so it tastes better. By noticing we also remember, so that year on year we can build a reference library in our minds of how plants perform in different conditions, and tend to them differently as necessary, helping us be more successful gardeners with happier plants.

Poppy (*Papaver rhoeas* Shirley Group)

"We see nothing truly till we understand it."

John Constable,

PAINTER

Constable's observation is the first step toward understanding plants. It is entirely possible to teach ourselves gardening purely from experience, but it behoves us to acknowledge that we do not – indeed cannot – know everything about horticulture. We must look at books, search the internet or ask friends and neighbours for advice every now and then. For understanding how plants work – even at a basic level – not only brings a new sense of appreciation to our gardening, but helps us care for them in a more informed way. Looking at a plant can tell us a lot about the kind of conditions it prefers: for example, the narrow silvery leaves of lavender indicate that it evolved in a hot, dry climate, where small leaves that reflect the sunlight helped minimize water loss. Such a shrub will therefore not appreciate being planted in a bog. On the other hand, the fine wide green leaves of a hosta tell us that it prefers dappled shade and a good moisture level in the soil – too much hot sun or not enough water and those thin leaves will start to fry. Many of our most celebrated gardeners talk about each individual plant they have as if they are close friends. They know their plants in minute detail, and appreciate them all the more for it.

Blue tit *(Cyanistes caeruleus)*
sitting in a cherry tree

Dealing with diseases and pests

It also helps to be fully aware in the garden when it comes to dealing with plant diseases. Removing the affected part – even if it is only a single leaf – of a plant when it first shows signs of infection can halt the problem in its tracks. Once it has got to the point at which even the most preoccupied gardener notices it, the plant is probably beyond help.

Pests are a slightly different matter. The other inhabitants of our gardens are numerous and varied, and many will prey on our plants, but before we lunge in with the bug spray or the boot to squash a slug, take a moment to think about your attitude toward it. Who has more right to be there, you or the pest? Who was there first? Are you getting rid of it purely out of squeamishness or fear? The caterpillars, aphids and birds that do so much damage to our precious plants have a place in the natural order of things, just as we and the plants do.

However, hanging out an "All pests welcome" sign on the garden gate is not likely to bring us much contentment, and will, of course, have a detrimental effect on our plants, so it comes down to a question of balance. Rather than spraying roses at the first sign of an aphid infestation, remember that it will take a few days for the population to be sufficiently large to attract the attention of birds, which will then come in and clear the plants for us. Learning about natural predators for the main garden pests, and what to plant and do in order to attract such predators, is an essential part of becoming a good gardener (see *A mindful garden for wildlife*, on pages 106–15). Try to aim for deterrence rather than destruction – it sits better, even if you do not believe in karma. For example, rather than using slug pellets, tidy up the pile of old pots that the slugs are hiding in during the day. The birds, and even amphibians, will come in and feast royally, removing your problem. Allow things to develop in their natural way and do not pile on the fertilizer, which creates lush but weak foliage – ideal fodder for aphids. Look on the bright side of damage: the plant that was grazed to the ground has come back, and flowered later and more bountifully than its neighbours, because each shoot has now produced two new ones.

A POSITIVE ATTITUDE

Attitude and motivation are crucial for successful gardening and mindfulness. There is no point in creating a garden if we do not enjoy maintaining it. A single pot plant is better than large herbaceous borders if the pot plant brings joy and the borders prove a chore-filled burden. The pleasant–unpleasant scale is a useful concept here. Gardens and gardening are pleasant, but it is possible to have too much of a good thing. When the scale starts to tip toward unpleasant it is time for a reassessment (where and when it tips is entirely personal). For example, the pot of nasturtiums planted last year was pleasant: the red and orange blooms brought colour to that corner of the garden, the bees loved it and the leaves, flowers and seeds were all delicious to eat. This year they have popped up all over the garden, the orange/red shades are clashing horribly with the pink roses and you are having to weed them all out: unpleasant. This is a superficial example, but the point can be applied to almost anything (a little chocolate cake: pleasant – too much chocolate cake: unpleasant), and it is worth being mindful of exactly what is enjoyable about gardening so that we do not turn something good into a chore.

Success at gardening and success at mindfulness take a consistent effort over a long period of time. An enthusiastic burst of hard work followed by a long period of disinterest will not produce the desired results. As illustrated above, it is much easier to make that effort if it is enjoyable, but there can be other reasons we do not want to do something. It is very easy to put off the garden, or mindfulness practice, because there are many more important things to do first, or it is just not the right time, or we are not sure what we are supposed to be doing. To counter all of these, a brief contemplation of impermanence can be helpful – not only our own impermanence but that of our garden. Putting off the watering for too long could mean a lot of dead plants. It will never be the perfect time, and any lack of confidence is also an impermanent state, easily rectified by recourse to the appropriate advice. That said, it is important to make sure that we also make time to enjoy our gardens, to stop for a cup of tea and spend a few mindful moments drinking in the experience of just being there.

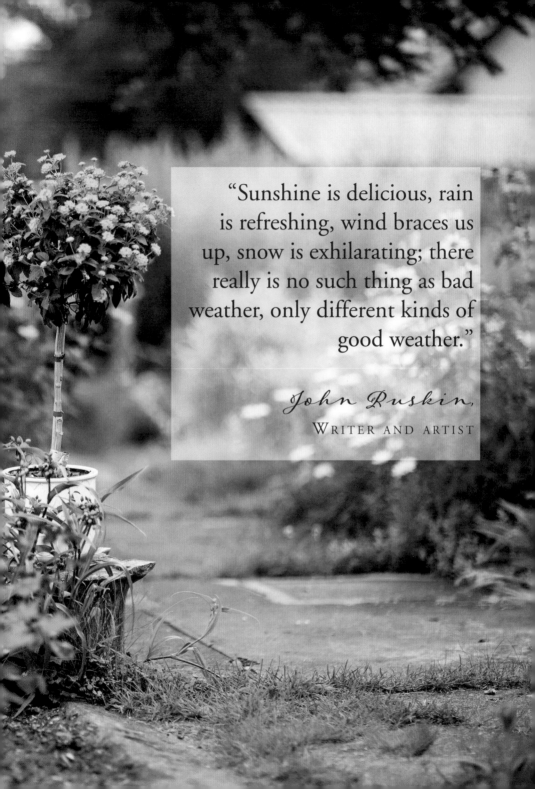

"Sunshine is delicious, rain is refreshing, wind braces us up, snow is exhilarating; there really is no such thing as bad weather, only different kinds of good weather."

John Ruskin,
WRITER AND ARTIST

This comment of John Ruskin's (see previous page) is oft-quoted, but it is worth repeating here because it illustrates how our attitude affects our outlook. If we can look positively on our garden – indeed, on life – and have a positive and long-term motivation to work in the garden, the hiccups and bumps along the way seem less significant. Our brains have a natural bias toward being negative, so it is easy to be dissatisfied with what we have, or our progress, but by looking at why we are doing something, rather than how much or little we have achieved, we can regain that enthusiasm. For example, a short-term goal of weeding a bare bed to make it look tidy for a friend's visit is not as good a motivation as weeding it knowing you are going to plant and sow lots of lovely vegetables or flowers that will bring pleasure in the months and years to come.

COPING WITH SETBACKS

It is often said that the true test of character is how we respond to our failures rather than our successes, and the garden is certainly a source of many potential failures. Some are not our fault – acts of God as the insurance

companies would call them – but the rest generally fall into errors of over- or under-cultivation. An over-cosseted plant is more susceptible to pest and disease infection, but a tender plant chucked into the ground without any hardening off will suffer a check to its growth. If we can chalk these mistakes up to experience and, rather than dwelling on them, continue through our mindfulness practice to focus on the present, we will go a long way toward being a better gardener.

Back to the senses

"Those who had so strenuously dwelt on the dirt and dangers of this route had said not a word about the beauties, the matchless beauties of the scenery."

William Cobbett,

RURAL RIDES

This comment from Cobbett's 1830 account of his travels around England is incredibly illustrative of how different people's points of view affect their perception of the same place. The local men who gave Cobbett directions were full of warnings about the bad road: it was a familiar journey for them and that familiarity had bred, if not contempt, then at least a lack of appreciation for the scenery's "matchless beauties". On the other hand Cobbett, travelling the road for the first time, saw not the mud and potential for landslides, but the fields, the hedges and the trees all coming together in one picturesque revelation. In other words, Cobbett was being mindful of his situation; the locals were not.

Bees are attracted to the brightly
coloured flowers of African
marigolds (*Tagetes erecta*)

In mindful practice we need an anchor to bring our focus back to every time our attention wanders. For sitting mindfulness practice this is the rise and fall of the breath, but in the garden we can use our senses as the anchor instead. Nature calls on all our senses in a garden, grounding us in the present moment, so that we are able not only to get off autopilot but also to free ourselves from the past and future worries. We can watch our thoughts pass by like bees flitting from flower to flower, and thus diminish their effects on our minds and bodies. The fact that we automatically tend to slow down our movements on entering a garden, stopping to look and just enjoy the sun on our face and the fresh air, is in itself halfway to a mindful state.

Imagine you are deadheading roses. It is a routine task, not particularly physically challenging or requiring a lot of concentration, and your mind wanders. You are still performing the task, but not paying full attention to it, and the initial thought that strayed across your mind has led you into getting caught up in worries about your pension. There is nothing you can do about the pension at that very moment, so there is no point in worrying about it. Indeed, the worrying only makes it worse, so bring the focus back to the roses. You might choose to focus on the colour of each flower as you cut it away, the feeling of squeezing the secateurs (hand pruners) in your hand, the scent of the roses around you or the sound of the bees buzzing in the open blooms. After making your selection, you then return to what you are doing in that very moment, and experience it fully. The worries move on. Your mind will wander again, it is in its nature to do this, but the garden is a place where you can come back to yourself again and again.

Deadheading roses – cut just above a
leaf axil a little way down the stem

Look on learning to be mindful as an opportunity to rekindle that childhood curiosity and openness to the wonder of things. As adults we fall all too easily into becoming blasé, disenchanted or even contemptuous about the natural world around us, especially if we were not brought up around plants. The shabby shrubs outside the office or grocery store can still be beautiful, even if pruned badly and full of weeds, when we look a little closer. The fact that they survive in those kinds of situations is in itself often a miracle, but if the overall appearance is not pleasing, look instead at a single leaf or flower. We are so often buried in our own business (and busy-ness) that stopping to look can rekindle a happiness, or stimulate a memory we thought we had lost. Having made that initial step, we can look afresh with new eyes and listen with new ears to see and hear the world around us.

The same is true of our gardens. We might feel that they are boring and tired, but try looking at them from a child's perspective. Lawns are more than just grass – they are football pitches where the greatest goal can be scored, or a sea full of monsters to navigate their imaginary boat through. Get up close, down low, with the plants and see the miniature world within them: the minibeasts doing battle, the new shoots breaking through buds.

The next time it starts raining when you are in the garden, do not rush for cover, stay out there and experience the weather. Get an umbrella and waterproof boots if you want, but just enjoy the refreshment for a while – splash in some puddles for the pure unbridled joy of it.

"You can even learn to handle slugs – if you make up your mind to do it. It is surprising how we can train ourselves, if we want to."

Christopher Lloyd,
CUTTINGS: A YEAR IN THE GARDEN

It is best to choose a single sense to focus on at any one time. Trying to absorb all that is happening around you, as well as what you are doing, will lead to a sensory overload, and the mind is more likely to seek peace in thoughts rather than senses. As George Eliot wrote in her novel *Middlemarch*, "it would be like hearing the grass grow and the squirrel's heart beat, and we should die of that roar". Later on in this book there are suggestions as to what you may choose to use as an anchor at each stage of the task (for example, see page 132). However, in general, anything with a good rhythm to it is a good start: for example, your feet hitting the ground as you walk; the snip of your secateurs (hand pruners) as you prune; or plucking raspberries one by one from the cane. Active tasks such as gardening are often much easier to return to than the breath, but as with all mindfulness it will take practice and patience.

Pausing on the threshold

At the risk of torturing the metaphor, it is really important to ground yourself before you start gardening. Rushing out of the door will not enhance a mindful state; therefore pause on the threshold. The following chapter has some suggestions on how the threshold itself can help bring the mind back into the body (see pages 66–125); use this section for guidance on how to start each of the exercises in *Mindful garden practices* (see pages 126–71) and *Mindful garden projects* (see pages 172–215), as well as any time you head out into the garden.

The time to pause is literally as you take that first step into the garden. Close the door or gate behind you, then stop. Find a spot ahead of you on which your eyes can rest, then take a deep breath, in through your nose and out through your mouth. As you breathe in, feel your chest expanding and the smell of the fresh air; as you breathe out, feel your shoulders and body relax and sink downward. Take several more deep breaths, focusing on the movement in your body as the air goes in and out. If you find it easier to concentrate on your nose or stomach rather than your chest, do just that – the aim is to feel the movement wherever it is strongest in your body.

Continue standing in the same spot and mentally scan your body from top to toe. It can be helpful to close your eyes. You are not looking for aches and pains, though they may become more apparent when you start to notice them, so try not to judge or criticize them ("my back hurts – I should not have picked up that heavy box yesterday without help"). Just peacefully move your attention down your body. Notice what does not hurt as well as what does. The intention is not to change anything, but simply to continue bringing the focus onto the senses and body rather than your thoughts. The body usually relaxes automatically once it realizes it is tense. If you get distracted, just bring the focus back and pick up where you left off. There is no time limit, but you will probably want to take a minute or two to do this.

Now it is time to move your attention to the world around you, starting with the weather. Feel the sun on your face, its warmth and brightness; or relish the rain. Is it large droplets, or a gentle drizzle? Is there a breeze or wind? Is the air cold or warm on your skin, dry or humid?

Open your eyes, if you have not already done so, and see the garden around you. Do not search for jobs to be done, for weeds or pests, but similarly do not look for the brightest and best flowers. You should simply be seeking to hone your senses, to notice. Drink in the images around you – of the garden and also of the wider landscape. Survey your surroundings and the sky, perhaps do a little cloud spotting – all too often we do not look up or out of our immediate bubble. Again, you do not need to spend a long time on this – you are just practising concentrating on the direct experience of the senses.

Move your focus to the sounds around you – be they birds singing or traffic roaring. Noises, particularly ever-present ones, are easy to tune out after a while, so really listen to everything you can hear both immediately around you and farther afield.

By now your body should have relaxed a little, and your mind warmed up to the mindfulness training you are about to embark on. Step forward knowing what it is you are going to do (whether it be a particular task, or just sitting and enjoying the garden more fully) and go about it with attentiveness and purpose.

The beauty of mindfulness practice is that it is impossible to get wrong. You may finish an exercise berating yourself for allowing your attention to wander too often, but the fact is that you noticed your attention wandering and brought it back each time, thereby strengthening those muscles in the brain. Even if it takes you several minutes, longer even, to realize you are caught up in your thoughts – and this is particularly easy with habitual actions – you do still notice and, every time you do, those neurons add another strand to their connection. Mentally narrating what you are doing is just as much thinking as worrying about paying the mortgage is, so try to live in the moment.

If you need to slow down your movements in order to focus properly on the senses during any of the exercises in this book, that is absolutely fine. The more you practise, the easier it will become. Indeed, if you would prefer to sit for the first deep breaths and body scanning, that too makes no difference, though ideally the seat would not be too far into the garden.

Remember, with all that you do in the garden, the aim is to experience it as fully as possible, to be completely present in the moment and not away with your thoughts.

"Let us, then, be up and doing,
With a heart for any fate;
Still achieving, still pursuing,
Learn to labour and to wait."

Henry Wadsworth Longfellow,
A PSALM OF LIFE

Mindful walking

After breathing, there are few actions more habitual than walking, and so with all mindfulness exercises it is good to bring your attention to bear on this activity as well. You are already walking: walking mindfully takes no more effort, but has many more benefits. Conveniently, too, it can be easily broken down into manageable chunks. You can start by being mindful for just the first few minutes, and add more as you get used to it. This means that it is easier to feel you have made progress and achieved something, which reinforces the positive wiring in your brain.

Walking mindfully can be a sobering experience to start with, as you realize how little you have actually noticed about the world around you, particularly if it is a walk you do often, such as to the shed or to work. How often have you arrived at your destination with no actual memory of how you got there? This is especially common with regular journeys such as the daily commute. However, do not let this get you down – you may not have noticed it before, but you are doing so now and that is the important part.

Alternatively, you may wonder why you should bother trying to be mindful when you are en route – the path you are walking never changes; it is just the same old plants, houses or stores every day. In reality there will be many changes to that landscape if only you paid closer attention and, even if a particular aspect has not changed, your mind is in a different mood today compared with yesterday, so you will see it differently.

A garden is the perfect place to walk mindfully, as it is generally a relatively quiet environment, which makes focusing easier. It is also full of myriad stimulations for your senses, and lovely things to look at, hear and smell. If you are concentrating on the sensory experience of your walk, smelling sweet flowers, listening to birdsong and admiring the way the dew glistens on the grass are probably preferable to contemplating the stink and roar of traffic. If your own garden is limited to a collection of pot plants on a windowsill or balcony, or it is so densely planted there is simply no space to walk, use a public garden or park instead. It is preferable to walk in a place where you can keep roughly the same pace for the whole experience, even if it is up and down or round and round the garden.

As with all mindfulness practice, walking mindfully should be an enjoyable experience. There is no need to walk in any particular way (although in the early stages concentrating on your body's movements can engender some self-consciousness, which gives the potential for falling over your own feet). Just relax and walk naturally.

Start by trying to incorporate a mindful walk into your day just once, perhaps that initial one into the garden, and build up from there. If you can – and again this is where walking in your own garden is a big advantage – walk barefoot. The direct contact with the ground enhances the feeling of the movement of walking, and you are more in touch with Nature that way, both literally and metaphorically.

Read this section through a couple of times, then leave the book behind as you go out and walk. Frequent practice, referring back to the text as necessary before each session, will soon fix the different stages in your memory. Do not worry if you forget a stage, the general principles are what are important here.

"Be happy in that moment, that is enough. Each moment is all we need, nothing more."

Mother Teresa,
SAINT, NUN AND
MISSIONARY

Before you start walking, take a moment to stop (see *Pausing on the threshold*, on page 55) in order to notice the space around you and specifically what you are standing on. Move the focus to your body, and feel the contact of your feet with the ground. As you become more aware of the weight of the body pressing down on the soles of your feet, notice how it is distributed. Are you standing more on your heels or toes? The inside of your feet or the outside? Take a moment to balance yourself so that you are standing roughly centred, with the weight balanced between heel and toe, inside and outside.

 Now start to walk – moving at your natural speed, whether that be slow or quick – maintaining that general awareness of the world around you, what you can see, hear and smell. After a minute or so, concentrate on the movements your body makes as you walk – your legs lifting and stepping forward, your arms swinging, perhaps your torso moving from side to side slightly, your head and neck as you look around. The aim is not to change how you walk or to do anything else, but just to notice your body's movements and where it comes into contact with the earth as you do so.

 Move the focus to just your legs. Feel the muscles tense and relax as you lift each one to step forward, and the switch between legs. Continue this for a few steps, then finally centre your attention on your feet. Notice how the weight feels as you move from heel to toe and then lift the foot off the ground. Also appreciate the pattern of tension and relaxation in each foot as it moves in turn. Carry on walking with the focus on the soles of your feet for as long as you want to. If you become distracted, as soon as you notice bring your attention back to the sensation of your movement, directly experiencing that rhythmic stepping from left to right and back again.

 Keep your focus on the steady stepping motion, but not to the extent that you exclude the world around you. The aim here is to rest your attention on the sensation of walking, so that you automatically have a broad awareness of the world around you.

 Once you have finished, draw a line under the experience rather than analyse your performance. Once it is done, it is done. However, make sure that you actively stop the exercise instead of just forgetting what you are supposed to be doing; in other words, finish on a period of being aware rather than being distracted and letting the practice fizzle out.

Where to meditate in the garden

Sometimes it is good to sit and focus on your breath for a while, rather than using the senses as an anchor for your mind, and the garden can be the perfect peaceful sanctuary in which to do this. The crucial point is to choose a spot with as few potential distractions as possible, where you will feel most comfortable. Whether it is in your own garden or a public place, use the following points to guide you to the right spot.

Garden meditation

 Find somewhere away from the beaten track (this is especially useful for public spaces), so that you will not be interrupted by people or animals coming up to you, or a ball being kicked into your legs by mistake.

 Choose somewhere in the shade during summer and in the sun during winter. Starting to feel too hot or cold halfway through your practice will take the focus away from the breath.

 Likewise, a sheltered spot in case of rain is better than out in the open, but if you are scared of spiders a covered structure in the garden may not be the best choice! Under the branches of a large tree is ideal.

 If you can, choose somewhere you can sit on the earth or grass (rather than on any man-made structure) or lean against a tree trunk. Whether or not you believe in a life force, this contact with natural surroundings is beneficial. If you are concerned about dirtying your clothes, a rug on the ground is still better than a bench.

 If a part of your garden or park has any particularly strong memories or emotions associated with it, consider whether it is the best place to meditate. If you can see the rose from your late grandfather's garden from where you are sitting, is it likely to draw your attention as you close your eyes and create more potential distraction in the mind?

"To sit in the shade on a fine day, and look upon verdure is the most perfect refreshment."

Jane Austen,
MANSFIELD PARK

The gardening community

Although the focus here has been on your personal experience of gardening, gardens are places of healing and sanctuary for many folk, and it is incredibly beneficial to your mental wellbeing to go out and connect with people.

You may wish to join your local gardening club or society, become more active in the running of your local allotment site or perhaps bring the joy of plants to more people with some urban planting (see *Further resources*, on pages 218–19). Perhaps you could just strike up a conversation with your neighbour over the garden fence. However you connect, a shared love of growing things is an ideal starting point to forge new friendships.

CHAPTER 3
Designing a mindful garden

Whether you are designing your entire garden from scratch, just making over a section, or adding and improving it over the years, there are a number of ways to make a space that will not only encourage active mindful practice, but also be a place for more passive relaxation. Later in this chapter are suggestions for good plants to use, and how to incorporate water and more wildlife in your garden (whether it be a large outdoor space or a windowsill), but before all of those considerations it is helpful to spend some time thinking about what you want your garden to be. Creating a mindful garden is not the same as making a therapeutic garden. It is about choosing plants that stimulate the senses. The following sections contain suggestions on incorporating plants for each of the senses (though, of course, they all interact in our brain, and a plant listed under scent may also have attractive flowers and textural leaves).

A mindful garden should also make you happy. First and foremost your garden is for you, and perhaps your family and close friends. It is not for your neighbours or passers-by because, while it is never a good idea to deliberately antagonize people with your plantings (an out-of-control Leyland cypress × *Cuprocyparis leylandii*, for example), no one else is living with your garden, or maintaining it. A garden is your personal space to unleash your creative impulses like an artist or to experiment like a scientist, or both. Do not use plants simply because they are suggested here as being good for encouraging mindfulness, but, on the other hand, be open to new ideas. You may think that you do not like fuchsias but there is such a huge range of plant types and sizes, with an even wider range of flower colours, that you might just find one you fancy. Take the time to look at and understand a plant before dismissing it out of hand on account of its name.

There are many places from which to seek inspiration for your garden. Bear in mind that the more you read about gardens and visit them, the more inspirational ideas you will find that you will want to include in your own space. Seeking new ideas need not put you out of pocket either, as there are plenty of green spaces that have free entry, while garden writing and photography are widely available on the internet. Your style and favourite plants are likely to change over the years that you garden, and quite probably from season to season too. This is all well and good: change is natural and being curious stops you from stagnating.

Armenian grape hyacinth
(*Muscari armeniacum*)

"Consult the Genius of the Place in all."

Alexander Pope,
POET AND ESSAYIST

Appreciating plant names

The history of plants is so long and complex that inevitably their names have accrued several connotations over the years. By considering some of these meanings when designing your garden you can in turn give your garden meaning too.

Firstly, there are plant botanical names. Some are purely descriptive, but others are named after certain people, events or their place of origin. Perhaps some of these things also have significance for you, so you may like to include them in your garden. For example, you might wish to bring back one of the many *Lampranthus* named after Tresco's Abbey Gardens to remind you of a particularly wonderful holiday in the Isles of Scilly.

Secondly, there is the language of flowers. We all know that red roses are associated with true love and lilies with funerals, but did you know that ornamental onions (*Allium*) stand for prosperity and fennel (*Foeniculum*) for strength? Other plants have special connotations too: for example, the Judas tree (*Cercis siliquastrum*) and yew (*Taxus baccata*) trees which are associated with graveyards.

Thirdly, and much more than any of these, is the importance or traditions that certain plants hold for you personally. Planting the same mock orange (*Philadelphus*) that your grandmother had growing in her garden (maybe even from a cutting from her plant) in your own garden is a wonderful way to remember her. Other plants are given as gifts, or are planted to mark special occasions such as births, marriages or deaths. These associations are not easily dismissed, and bring true importance to a garden. (See *Further resources*, on pages 218–19, for where to get more information on the meanings of plant names.)

Taking stock

You probably have a long list of plants you want to include in your garden, so it is time to rein in some of those ambitions. Remember that gardening is much easier when you are working with Nature rather than against it. You are much more likely to succeed if you are flexible in your approach and accommodate the peculiarities and microclimates of your particular garden, rather than forcing your ideas onto the land. Mimic the natural environment of your plants as closely as possible, and they will thrive. Plants (and humans) only become unhappy when compelled to live in an unsustainable situation. So, while you design your garden with your heart, you should plant it with your head, and inject some practicality as well.

The longer you spend creating your garden (although really it is a process that never ends), the more you appreciate it, and the more easily you see what does and does not do well. You can then adjust your plans accordingly. Ideally, in fact, when you first acquire a new garden, you should spend a year just observing it – where the sun falls in summer and winter and through the day, which areas of lawn get boggy when it rains, how that corner of the patio is a real heat trap. This knowledge is invaluable when you come to put in beds, paths and plants of your own.

The renowned English garden designer Rosemary Verey was herself entirely self-taught, and over the years she came to understand the essentials: a garden must look inviting at any time of year; it should always include an element of surprise; that keeping a plan simple is often the best policy; and that it is important to get to know your plants, so that you are able to "choose them to suit their sites as well as their neighbours".

Design considerations

If you have the luxury of being able to design your whole garden from scratch, it can be helpful to consider how you will walk through it. Being able to see the entire space from the back door offers no mystery, and no pull to get you to the other end of the site. By dividing the garden into rooms, and obscuring some parts with trees, hedges, trellis or other living screens (such as a woven willow fence), you will see the garden unfold gradually as you walk through it, and there will always be something new to see, smell or touch. When designing imagine that you are creating a tour of your garden for friends: where would you like the main stopping points to be, the focal features? Make sure you also include space for relaxing and enjoying the garden – benches, places to eat, a lawn for chairs – as well as areas for other uses (bike storage and soccer pitches might not be your ideal now, but remember that those needs will change over the years). Finally, remember that you will not always be looking at the garden when you are in it – how will it appear from inside, both down and upstairs?

Committing your designs to paper is the best method (until you break ground anyway) of making sure that everything will eventually work in your garden. You do not need a degree in landscape surveying or to be a brilliant artist for this. Just sketch out your thoughts, preferably in a notebook that you can continue to add to over the years, with diary notes, observations and plant names too if you like. If you are daunted by this, remember that you are not being judged by anyone but yourself (and that mindfulness helps mute that internal critic for a while).

Start small if you are nervous, but also bear in mind that even great designers make errors. While there is the potential for mistakes, this is also a huge opportunity for you and your garden. Seize it, and create the best garden for you.

Planting for the senses

SIGHT

Professional garden designers utilize all sorts of visual trickery to transform their clients' gardens. Many of these are very simple, and easily adopted by the home gardener. One such is to plant in groups of odd numbers, unless even numbers are required for symmetry: for example, a climber on either side of a door. A select group of different plant types planted in large groups will make a garden look bigger than a mishmash of single plants. Other tricks for unifying a garden include repeated elements, such as the same shrub in several places around the garden, or the now-classic balls of box (*Buxus*) at intervals down the front of a mixed border, and using a limited colour palette for each season.

Colour is the most obvious aspect of what we see in the garden, but a garden does not have to be a riot of colour to be suitable for mindfulness. The point of being mindful in the garden is that we see even the tiniest flower, or the way one leaf casts a shadow on another, as well as that border of orange marigolds (*Tagetes*). Indeed, we could plant a garden created entirely in shades of green. Colours can greatly affect the way we feel, but each is deeply personal. The cool colours (blues, purples, greens) are for many calming and relaxing (it is why many dentists' waiting rooms are green), but they may make others feel sad. A hot palette of reds, oranges and yellows can appear warm and welcoming to some, but for others their passion is too close to anger. Within each colour there are also many variations to be observed. Hostas – plants generally grown more for their foliage than their flowers – are a good example of the range of a single colour. Though all the varieties' leaves are green, some are yellow-green, while others are blue-green.

Yellow mulleins (*Verbascum*) and white foxgloves (*Digitalis*) add height to a colourful border that also includes *Artemisia*, *Knautia*, *Salvia* and *Sysirinchium*

"Beauty in things exists in the mind which contemplates them."

David Hume,
OF THE STANDARD OF TASTE AND OTHER ESSAYS

"Of course we made many mistakes…
As it was, I planted all the wrong things and
planted them in the wrong places."

Vita Sackville-West,
GARDEN DESIGNER AND WRITER

To keep a garden feeling spacious and cool, limit the use of hot colours to no more than 20 per cent of the overall palette. Placing the hot colours at the front of the garden (closest to the house) and the cool ones at the back also creates a sense of distance and the impression of size. However, to make a place feel smaller, we can put some hot colours at the back. For those who are only at home and able to enjoy their garden in the evenings, include many more white and pale-flowered plants so that they will be easier to see in the dusk. White plants are often pollinated by night-time insects because they are so visible in the dark, and are often scented only at night as well. Finally, remember that colour in plants is not limited to the flowers and leaves – there are coloured stems and trunks too.

Beyond colour, there are other things you will see – a plant's form, for example. Is it upright or prostrate, tall or squat, weeping or cascading, billowing or skinny? Is it columnar, dense or open? How are the leaves shaped – and the flowers? What does the texture look like (as opposed to feel like – see *Touch*, on pages 95–97)? Does it appear solid or feathery, shiny or matt, rough or smooth? How does the plant look different in the light and shade, and as the plant moves?

Elements of the garden's appearance to consider include not just the individual plants but also how they will combine with their immediate neighbours and work with the overall effect. You will be looking very closely at your garden when viewing it mindfully, so give yourself plenty to see. The plants on the following pages provide a few good examples, including those with really obvious features and something to draw your attention in every season, but there are, of course, many hundreds of thousands of plants to choose from, and all are worth planting.

Plants for sight

ORNAMENTAL GARDEN
Trees
Acer palmatum (Japanese maple)

Amelanchier lamarckii (snowy mespilus)

Arbutus unedo (strawberry tree)

Betula utilis var. *jacquemontii* (West
   Himalayan birch)

Catalpa bignonioides (Indian bean tree)

Eucalyptus gunnii (cider gum)

Liquidambar styraciflua (sweet gum)

Liriodendron tulipifera (tulip tree)

Nyssa sylvatica (black gum, tupelo)

Pyrus salicifolia 'Pendula' (weeping silver pear)

Salix (willow)

Climbers
Clematis cirrhosa (evergreen clematis)

Cobaea scandens (cup and saucer plant)

Humulus lupulus 'Aureus' (golden hop)

Passiflora caerulea (blue passion flower)

Wisteria sinensis (Chinese wisteria)

Left to right: *Passiflora caerulea* (blue
passion flower); *Acer palmatum* (Japanese
maple); Swiss chard 'Bright Lights'

Shrubs

Artemisia ludoviciana (western mugwort)

Buddleja globosa (orange ball tree)

Callicarpa bodinieri var. *giraldii* 'Profusion' (beauty berry)

Camellia

Cornus alba 'Sibirica' (Siberian dogwood), *C. kousa* var. *chinensis* (Chinese dogwood)

Corylus avellana 'Contorta' (corkscrew hazel)

Hydrangea paniculata

Magnolia stellata (star magnolia)

Rubus thibetanus (ghost bramble)

Herbaceous perennials, grasses and bulbs

Acanthus spinosus (bear's breeches)

Allium cristophii (star of Persia)

Crocosmia 'Lucifer' (monbretia)

Cyclamen coum (eastern cyclamen, *C. hederifolium* (ivy-leaved cyclamen)

Dahlia

Erigeron karvinskianus (Mexican fleabane)

Fritillaria meleagris (snake's head fritillary)

Galanthus nivalis (common snowdrop)

Helleborus niger (Christmas rose)

Hemerocallis (daylily)

Heuchera (coral flower)

Hosta (plantain lily)

Houttuynia cordata 'Chameleon' (heart-leaved houttuynia)

Iris

Meconopsis grandis (Himalayan blue poppy)

Melianthus major (honey bush)

Ophiopogon planiscapus 'Nigrescens' (black mondo)

Phlomis russeliana (Turkish sage)

Phormium tenax (New Zealand flax)

Pulsatilla vulgaris (pasque flower)

Sempervivum (houseleek)

Stipa gigantea (golden oats)

Annuals and biennials

Amaranthus caudatus (love-lies-bleeding)

Brassica oleracea (ornamental cabbage)

Cleome (spider flower)

Cosmos bipinnatus 'Purity' (cosmea)

Helianthus annuus (sunflower)

Lunaria annua (honesty)

Nigella damascena (love-in-a-mist)

Tagetes erecta (African marigold), *T. patula* (French marigold)

Thunbergia alata Susie Series (black-eyed-Susan)

KITCHEN GARDEN
Trees

Malus × *moerlandsii* 'Profusion' (crab apple)

Perennials

Angelica archangelica (angelica)

Artichoke 'Green Globe'

Cynara cardunculus (cardoon)

Physalis peruviana (Cape gooseberry)

Rhubarb

Annuals and biennials

Beetroot/beet 'Chioggia'

Borago officinalis (borage)

Borlotti bean 'Lingua di Fuoco 2'

Broad/fava bean 'Crimson Flowered'

Broccoli 'Romanesco'

Cabbage 'Red Drumhead'

Calendula officinalis (pot marigold)

Courgette/zucchini 'Tromboncino d'Albenga'

French/green bean 'Cosse Violette'

Swiss chard 'Bright Lights'

Tropaeolum majus (nasturtium)

SCENT

When you are caught up in your own thoughts, it is easy to look without seeing and to hear without listening, but it is harder to ignore a fragrance. Imagine you are walking along a busy street. You are returning from an important meeting that did not go well, and your mind is a runaway train of the potential consequences. Your eyes are cast downward to your phone, or the radio plays in your headphones. Suddenly your attention is caught by a delicious scent: honeysuckle (*Lonicera*). You stop to look at the plant, which is draping over a garden fence. You catch a flower in your hand and cup it to your nose, feeling the soft petals against your fingers and breathing deeply to catch the fragrance. You hear the bees in the nearby flowers and the change in tone of their buzzing as they move toward the nectar; you look at the way the stems are twining around each other, and at the soft green of the leaves. You are totally focused in that moment on the experience of your senses – all else is let go.

All gardens have the potential to utilize some form of scent, and taking a moment to really breathe that in is an opportunity to refocus the attention of the mind on the present. Sometimes we cannot avoid the smell – it fills the air, making us notice it whether we like it or not. We really have to get up close to other fragrances, such as the delicate honeyed tones of the crocus flower. Sometimes it is not possible to locate the source of a fragrance, and searching it out makes us notice all the plants around us properly; the scent of other plants rubs off on our fingers and is a reminder for the rest of the day to bring us back to the present.

Far more than what we see and hear, our sense of smell triggers strong emotions, and particularly memories. This is because the part of the brain responsible for processing scents is strongly linked with the parts of the brain responsible for memories and feelings. This can be a mixed blessing in

Rosa 'Céline Forestier' and honeysuckle
(*Lonicera*) make a fragrant pairing

a mindful garden: strong scents are brilliant for helping us stay focused in the present, but, if they also spark memories, it is easier for the brain to get caught up in thinking again. However, do not avoid using certain favourite scented plants simply for this reason – just be aware of their potential effect, or avoid that area of the garden if you are particularly prone to distraction that day.

Scent in the garden could be a mixture of a number of different plants or there could be one predominant one. (It is best not to put all the strongly scented plants together, or it can become a bit overpowering.) Floral scents are obvious, but they have many different elements within them to be discovered, and there are herbaceous smells as well. Some are intensified when you touch them or get up close, while others are best left to fill the air with fragrance.

Placing scented plants next to paths or near the house is always a good idea, especially for winter-flowering shrubs that you might not otherwise be able to get close to in a wet season. Summer scents could be incorporated near seating or even in seating, as in the case of a chamomile seat – the best chamomile variety to use is *Chamaemelum nobile* 'Treneague' because it is low-growing and non-flowering. Make it easy to reach a small plant with a delicious scent, by planting it in a pot or at least at the edge of a border.

Although flowers are often highly scented, leaves should not be ignored – don't focus only on the culinary herbs either. The crushed autumn leaves of sweet gum (*Liquidambar styraciflua*) smell like mangoes, and those of the katsura tree (*Cercidiphyllum japonicum*) like burned sugar. Freshly cut grass, summer rain evaporating off hot stone and sweet basil (*Ocimum basilicum*) on a sunny windowsill are all scents that do not need a large or densely planted garden. Of course, smells in the garden are not always pleasant – such as rotting vegetation, a bucket of standing water or a pack of old fertilizer – yet they do not have to be pleasant to serve as a sensory anchor, something to bring your thoughts back to the task at hand.

The following pages suggest some scented plants, but there are many more. Look for words such as "odorata" or "fragrantissima" in the plant name, as these will indicate that it is scented in some way. If you are not sure you will like a scent, source the plant when it is in flower so you can try before you buy.

Plants for scent

ORNAMENTAL GARDEN

Trees

Calocedrus decurrens (incense cedar)
Cercidiphyllum japonicum (katsura tree)
Cladrastis kentukea (yellow wood)
Liquidambar styraciflua (sweet gum)
Magnolia yunnanensis
Tilia (lime)

Climbers

Clematis (virgin's bower)
Jasminum officinale (common jasmine)
Lonicera periclymenum 'Graham Thomas',
   L.p. 'Heaven Scent' (honeysuckle)

Left to right: *Lathyrus odoratus* 'Black Knight'
(sweet pea); *Rosa* Gertrude Jekyll 'Ausbord';
Tomatoes; *Helichrysum italicum* (curry
plant); *Convallaria majalis* (lily-of-the-valley)

Shrubs

Calycanthus floridus (Carolina allspice)
Camellia
Chimonanthus praecox (wintersweet)
Choisya ternata (Mexican orange blossom)
Daphne bholua (Nepalese paper plant)
Hamamelis (witch hazel)
Helichrysum italicum (curry plant)
Lonicera fragrantissima (winter-flowering honeysuckle)
Philadelphus maculatus P. 'Belle Étoile', 'Mexican
   Jewel' (mock orange)
Rosa R. Gertrude Jekyll ('Ausbord'), *R.* Margaret Merrill
   ('Harkuly'), *R. rugosa*, 'William Lobb' (rose)
Sarcococca confusa (Christmas box)
Styrax japonicus (Japanese snowbell)
Syringa meyeri 'Palibin' (lilac)
Viburnum × *bodnantense* 'Charles Lamont' (arrow
   wood), *V.* × *juddii*

Herbaceous perennials, grasses and bulbs

Actaea simplex Atropurpurea Group 'James Compton' (baneberry)
Convallaria majalis (lily-of-the-valley)
Cosmos atrosanguineus (chocolate plant)
Dianthus (pinks, carnations)
Hyacinthus orientalis (hyacinth)
L. 'Muscadet', *Lilium regale* (lily)
Monarda didyma (bergamot)
Narcissus (daffodil)
Phlox paniculata (perennial phlox)
Polianthes tuberosa 'The Pearl' (tuberose)
Viola odorata (sweet violet)

Annuals and biennials

Hesperis matronalis (sweet rocket)
Lathyrus odoratus (sweet pea)
Lobularia maritima 'Snowdrift' (sweet alyssum)
Matthiola incana (stock)
Nemesia 'Wisley Vanilla'
Nicotiana sylvestris (flowering tobacco)

KITCHEN GARDEN
Trees and shrubs

Citrus spp. (lemon/lime/orange trees)
Lavandula angustifolia (English lavender)
Rosmarinus officinalis (rosemary)
Sambucus nigra (common elder)

Perennials

Aloysia citrodora (lemon verbena)
Chamaemelum nobile 'Treneague' (lawn chamomile)
Melissa officinalis (lemon balm)
Mentha × *piperita* (peppermint)
Pelargonium (scented geranium)
Thymus vulgaris (common thyme)

Annuals and biennials

Carrots
Ocimum basilicum (sweet basil)
Tomatoes

"As I entered – mosses hushing
Stole all noises from my foot;
And a green elastic cushion,
Clasped within the linden's root,
Took me in a chair of silence, very rare
and absolute."

*Elizabeth Barrett
Browning,*

THE LOST BOWER

SOUND

Although gardens are often thought of as peaceful, quiet places, there is often
a symphony playing if we tune our ears to it. The plants, wildlife and weather
are all making noise around us – it might not be loud, but there is always
some sound in the garden to act as a sensory anchor and bring our focus back
to the present.

Sometimes the garden can be full of unwanted sounds such as noise from a
busy road or vocal neighbours. Planting and hard landscaping can help to
reduce the effects of such noise and provide a restful garden for all to enjoy.
The first step is to reflect and deflect as much noise as possible. This is done
using hard surfaces such as walls and fences that can bounce the sound
waves back toward their origin, so introduce these where possible around
the outside of the garden boundary. Soft surfaces absorb the sound waves
that do get into the garden. Trees and shrubs around the edges, especially

if underplanted, form a dense screen that will absorb a lot of noise. Plant evergreens where possible to ensure the level of protection is the same no matter what the season. Having a lawn rather than a patio will reduce the noise effects again, as will growing climbers against any house walls that face the garden.

The final step is to create sources of white noise in the garden, which will constantly mask the unwanted sounds and give you something else to focus on. Water is an excellent source of pleasant white noise. Water features are not just for masking unwanted noise, however; they are beautiful in their own right, and offer a range of sounds, from a gentle burble to a loud splashing. Even tiny courtyards can incorporate a bucket pond with fountain, but the larger the water feature, the more white noise it can create. Rustling trees and shrubs, such as the American, or quaking, aspen (*Populus tremuloides*), and bamboos are also good choices (see *Plants for sound*, on pages 92–93). The sound of wind chimes can be added to the garden as well, if desired. The more pleasant sounds that can be created to drown out the unpleasant ones, the better. This also extends to gardening – it is preferable to do a job by hand rather than using a machine if possible, so that we can be more aware of the world around us and not just a noisy engine.

The weather has a huge impact on the type and volume of sound in the garden. Most plants make noise in the wind as it rustles their leaves, rattles seed pods and blows fruit and nuts to the ground. Some move better than others, such as aspens (*Populus tremula*), grasses and bamboos. In autumn and winter, fallen leaves on the ground can eddy around courtyards, or provide crunchy fun to walk through and kick up, and a beech (*Fagus*) hedge will rustle its old leaves all winter before shedding them in favour of new ones in spring. Higher winds can also cause branches to creak or thump against fences and walls. Rain is soundless until it hits something – listen to the differences between a heavy and light shower, and the drops falling on different surfaces: a table, patio, grass, foliage, wet and dry soils.

Other plants may themselves be relatively quiet, but attract a range of noisy insects that buzz and click all day (and sometimes all night) long. Again, listen to the different pitches of the hum of insects' wings; from the delicate hoverfly to the large-winged dragonflies, beetles and flies, they all make distinct sounds. A large bumblebee droning directly past your ear can feel as loud as a jumbo jet if you are not expecting it. Birds lend us their song and, by being mindful of them in the garden, we can learn the songs of different species. We may even be lucky enough to have some amphibians such as frogs and toads hiding in the undergrowth or living in a pond. Listen for their croaks, and especially for their high-pitched squeaks that indicate they have been disturbed, albeit accidentally.

Finally, we can tune into the noises that we make ourselves in the garden – the snip of the secateurs (hand pruners), the scratching of the rake or the pop of a pea pod as we sneak a snack from the vegetable garden. Hard landscaping (paths, walls, any feature that is not planted) can provide an array of sounds as well – our steps ring out on paving, but crunch on gravel.

The more practised we get at being mindful in the garden, the easier it will become to hear all the wonderful sounds of Nature around us. It may help to just stand or sit and close the eyes for a minute or two at first. Eliminating the sense of sight automatically heightens our other senses. The following list includes plants that are particularly noisy in themselves – for those that attract birds and insects, see *Planting for birds*, *Planting for bees* and *Planting for butterflies and moths*, on pages 112, 113 and 114.

Plants for sound

ORNAMENTAL GARDEN
Trees

Aesculus hippocastanum (horse chestnut)

Populus tremula (aspen), *P. tremuloides*
(American aspen)

Salix. x sepulcralis var. *chrysocoma* (golden
weeping willow)

Left to right: *Populus tremula* (aspen); *Garrya
elliptica* (silk tassel bush); *Aquilegia vulgaris*
(columbine); *Nigella damascena* (love-in-a-mist);
Miscanthus sinensis 'Morning Light' (eulalia)

Climbers

Garrya elliptica (silk tassel bush)

Ipomoea (morning glory)

Shrubs

Chusquea culeou (Chilean bamboo)

Corylus avellana (hazel)

Fagus sylvatica (common beech – as a hedge)

Phyllostachys nigra (black bamboo)

Herbaceous perennials, grasses and bulbs

Aquilegia vulgaris (common columbine)

Baptisia australis (false indigo)

Cortaderia selloana (pampas grass)

Miscanthus sinensis 'Morning Light' (eulalia)

Molinia caerulea subsp. *arundinacea* (purple moor grass)

Pennisetum alopecuroides (Chinese fountain grass)

Stipa tenuissima (Mexican feather grass)

Annuals and biennials

Briza maxima (greater quaking grass)

Digitalis purpurea (common foxglove)

Nigella damascena (love-in-a-mist)

Papaver somniferum (opium poppy)

KITCHEN GARDEN
Annuals and biennials

Peas

Sweetcorn

TOUCH

Touch is the only sense that we can feel all over our body, though the receptors are concentrated in places such as our tongue, neck, feet and hands. The density of nerve endings in our fingertips is such that there is only around 3mm (⅛in) between them, whereas nerve endings can be up to 7cm (2½in) apart on other parts of the body such as the back. Through our skin we can determine texture, temperature and, of course, pressure and pain. As with the sounds in the garden, it can help (at all times but certainly in the early stages of learning to be mindful) to touch plants and other objects with the eyes closed, to heighten awareness of how they feel. Looking at an object at the same time can mean we are more dismissive of how it feels; that is, if we can see a leaf is rough we do not have to concentrate so hard on feeling the surface to determine this fact, and we might miss that it is actually densely hairy and feels rough only when stroked in one direction.

"There is not a sprig of grass that shoots uninteresting to me."

Thomas Jefferson,
THE LETTERS OF THOMAS JEFFERSON

Many plants in the garden invite themselves to be touched: we run our hand through grasses, or stroke fluffy lambs' ears (*Stachys byzantina*). Peeling, smooth or knobbly bark, rough or paper-thin leaves, silky velvety petals and even sharp thorns can all be tempting to touch. Sometimes we must wear gloves to protect ourselves – the scratching stems of cleavers (*Galium aperine*) can leave red welts on the skin, and we all know the pain of brushing against stinging nettles (*Urtica dioica*) – but if possible leave gloves off when among the plants, so that all the textures in the garden can be fully experienced.

Other plants bring out the child in us – a snapdragon (*Antirrhinum majus*) flower can be manipulated to look like snapping jaws. In times gone by, few could resist popping the seedheads of Himalayan balsam (*Impatiens glandulifera*), which can fire its seeds up to 7m (23ft) away, but as it is now known to be such an invasive weed we must refrain.

Some plants are themselves sensitive to touch, such as the sensitive plant (*Mimosa pudica*), which folds up its leaves at the slightest tap, like a shy debutante suddenly thrust into the limelight. The obedient plant (*Physostegia virginiana*) is so called because it will stay where it is put when bent, while the Venus flytrap (*Dionaea muscipula*) snaps its jaws shut when triggered by a fly.

As with scented plants, particularly tactile specimens should be put within reach (though avoid spiky and thorny plants along pathways). Many grasses make excellent "full stops" at the end of a border, while other plants are low-growing and so suitable for pots or the front of a bed.

When choosing a path surface, consider what it will be like to walk on, as well as how it will look. If you enjoy the feeling of lying on grass, or just running your hand over its springy surface, make sure you include some space for lawn in your garden design – somewhere that will get both shade and sun so that both temperatures can be experienced. Consider also what different surfaces are like to sit on – does that seat need to be a fabricated bench, or could you just use that old tree trunk instead? It is more texturally interesting.

The features that make a plant especially inviting to touch – smooth, fleshy leaves or soft downy ones – are often a result of the adaptations it has evolved to suit its habitat (in these two instances, minimizing water loss). By touching a plant we look closer at it, and in developing this greater understanding we become better gardeners as a result. The following plants (on pages 98–99) may have furry leaves, papery bark or silky flowers, but all possess at least one feature that will attract attention, and all are especially tactile. Those that are not fully hardy are marked with an asterisk (*).

Plants to touch

ORNAMENTAL GARDEN
Trees
Acer davidii (snake-bark maple), *A. griseum* (paperbark maple)
Betula nigra (river birch)
Prunus serrula (Tibetan cherry)

Left to right: *Acer griseum* (paperbark maple); *Alchemilla mollis* (lady's mantle); *Clematis vitalba* (old man's beard); *Liatris spicata* (button snakewort); Kale 'Cavolo Nero'

Climbers
Clematis 'Bill MacKenzie' (virgin's bower), *C. vitalba* (old man's beard)

Shrubs
Citrus trifoliata (Japanese bitter orange)
Euonymus alatus (winged spindle tree)
Hibiscus syriacus (rose of Sharon)
Salix caprea (goat willow)

Herbaceous perennials, grasses and bulbs (*not fully hardy)
Alchemilla mollis (lady's mantle)

Dionaea muscipula (Venus flytrap)

Liatris spicata (button snakewort)

Mimosa pudica (sensitive plant)*

Ornamental gourds (Cucurbita)

Pennisetum alopecuroides (Chinese
    fountain grass)

Phlomis fruticosa (Jerusalem sage)

Physostegia virginiana (obedient plant)

Salvia argentea (silver sage)

Stachys byzantina (lambs' ears)

Stipa pennata (feather grass)

Annuals and biennials

Antirrhinum majus (snapdragon)

Lagurus ovatus (hare's tail grass)

Limonium sinuatum (sea lavender, statice)

KITCHEN GARDEN
Trees and climbers

Grapes

Kiwis

Peaches

Perennials

Sea kale

Annuals and biennials

Broccoli 'Romanesco'

Florence fennel

Kale 'Cavolo Nero'

Taste

Using the sense of taste to focus the attention is obviously useful in the kitchen garden (whether it be a veg garden, allotment, growing bag of tomatoes, or even just a few herbs on the windowsill), yet many ornamental plants are also edible, so it is possible to apply this sense when wandering around most gardens. Taste covers not just whether something is sweet, sour, salty, bitter or savoury (the elusive umami flavour), but also its temperature and texture in your mouth. It is the sense that is most closely linked to the other senses, especially smell. A large proportion of the taste of something is actually informed by what it smells like, and you probably remember doing experiments at school where you ate something while holding your nose.

Everyone has the space to grow something edible. If you do not have a garden, use a windowsill to house a couple of pots of herbs. Many fruits and vegetables can also be grown in pots. In fact, seed and plant merchants are continually breeding new varieties more suitable for pot-growing, in recognition that many people who want to grow food do not have much garden space.

> "My friend, the things that do attain
> The happy life be these, I find:
> The riches left not got with pain;
> The fruitful ground, the quiet mind."

Henry Howard,
THE MEANS TO ATTAIN HAPPY LIFE

Many vegetables and herbs can be easily grown from seed, making them inexpensive plants as well. There is much debate over whether home-grown food tastes better than store-bought. For some crops – staples such as onions, for example – the answer is probably no, but for others, especially those that really benefit from being harvested ripe and/or eaten as soon as possible after picking, the answer is undoubtedly yes, for most gardeners. What is most relevant for the mindful gardener is the fact that eating a home-grown fruit or vegetable is more likely to encourage mindful eating (that is, really paying close attention to the food and its taste, as opposed to a TV dinner). We do not want just to wolf it down; we prefer to savour it because we put time and effort into growing it. Having edible plants in the garden also gives us another opportunity to bring our attention back to the present with our senses: if we are weeding the fruit and vegetable garden and our attention wanders, the taste of a perfectly ripe, sun-warmed strawberry will bring the mind back to the here and now in the most delicious way.

Fruit and vegetable plants need not be limited to a dedicated space in the garden – they can be incorporated into ornamental plantings as well. A wigwam of climbing beans is a great way to add height to a border, and fruit bushes can be used in place of other shrubs – blueberries in particular have wonderful autumn foliage as well as fruit and floral interest. Try using vegetables in place of summer bedding plants. Fortunately, herbs are pretty plants in their own right, as well as useful in the kitchen. With a little planning, and by including ornamental plants that are also edible (see *Plants to taste*, on pages 104–105), there could be beds and borders brimming with delicious things to eat and something to savour every few steps (though try to save some for the kitchen!).

In addition to mainstream edible plants and some ornamental ones, many weeds are also edible, but, as many require cooking first, they are not necessarily going to serve as sensory anchors. Daisy (*Bellis perennis*) petals can be scattered in salads, fat hen (*Chenopodium album*) and nettles (*Urtica dioica*) can be cooked like spinach, and dandelion (*Taraxacum officinale*) flowers make a delicious jelly, to name but a few. (See *Further resources*, on pages 218–19, for more information on cooking with and eating weeds.)

Listed here are only those plants that are particularly good for picking and eating raw while in the garden. Those appearing under the ornamental garden heading either have edible flowers, fruit or leaves marked (F), (Fr) and (L), respectively, that can be eaten raw. There are other ornamental plants that are edible but require cooking – see *Further resources*, on pages 218–19 for more information on this. However, do be sure that what you are about to eat is edible because many other garden plants are poisonous – though rarely in small quantities. If you are pregnant or have health conditions, check that each plant is safe before eating it. All culinary herbs have edible flowers as well as leaves.

Plants to taste

ORNAMENTAL GARDEN
Key:
(F) = edible flowers
(Fr) = edible fruit
(L) = edible leaves

Trees
Amelanchier (Fr)
Syringa vulgaris (lilac) (F)

Climbers
Akebia quinata (chocolate vine) (Fr)

Left to right: *Centaurea cyanus* (cornflower);
Acca sellowiana (pineapple guava); walnut;
cherries; *Perilla frutescens* (beef steak plant)

Shrubs
Acca sellowiana (pineapple guava) (F)
Fuchsia (Fr)
Lonicera caerulea (blue-berried honeysuckle) (Fr)
Rubus phoenicolasius (Japanese wineberry) (Fr)

Herbaceous perennials, grasses and bulbs
Agastache foeniculum (anise hyssop) (L)
Alcea rosea (hollyhock) (F, petals only)
Campanula versicolor, C. persicifolia,
   C. latifolia (bellflower) (L)
Chrysanthemum (F)
Dianthus (pinks) (F)
Gladiolus (F, petals only)
Hemerocallis (daylily) (F)
Monarda didyma (bergamot) (L, F)
Nepeta cataria (catmint) (F)
Phlox paniculata (perennial phlox) (F)

Primula vulgaris (primrose) (F)
Sanguisorba minor (salad burnet) (young L)
Tulipa (tulip) (F)
Yucca (Adam's needle) (F, petals only)

Annuals and biennials
Calendula officinalis (pot marigold) (F)
Centaurea cyanus (cornflower) (F)
Impatiens walleriana (busy Lizzie) (F)
Oenothera biennis (evening primrose) (F)
Perilla frutescens (beef steak plant) (F, L)
Salvia sclarea (biennial clary sage) (F)
Tropaeolum majus (nasturtium) (F, L)
Viola (F)

KITCHEN GARDEN
Trees and climbers
Apples
Apricots
Cherries
Figs
Grapes
Hazelnuts/cobnuts

Mulberries
Peaches and nectarines
Plums
Walnuts

Perennials
Blackberries and hybrid berries
Black currants
Blueberries
Raspberries
Red currants and white currants
Strawberries

Annuals and biennials
Carrots
Cucamelons
Cucumbers
Mangetout and sugar snap peas
Peas
Radishes (and seed pods)
Salad leaves
Tomatoes

A mindful garden for wildlife

The benefits of wildlife in a mindful garden

Taking time to sit and watch the wildlife in our garden is an excellent way
to be mindful. We can focus our attention on the activities of the birds on
the bird feeder, of the bees buzzing from flower to flower or of the butterfly's
erratic flight plan, and in those moments be completely present in the garden.
Watching wildlife helps us to feel connected with the wider world around
us, and that our garden is part of the natural environment. We can see who
comes and goes with different seasons, and mark their first appearances as
a harbinger of spring. The more we plant to encourage wildlife, the greater
the diversity of birds, bees, bugs and more we will attract, and learning to
identify these creatures involves us more closely with our gardens too.

"Sometimes I sits and thinks,
and then again I just sits."

author unknown,
PUNCH MAGAZINE, 1906

A large cabbage white butterfly
(*Pieris brassicae*) on English lavender
(*Lavandula angustifolia*)

Watching the birds and bees go about their daily business can be fascinating. The (literal) pecking order at the bird feeder, a bee getting increasingly covered in pollen as it goes from flower to flower and a wasp peeling off minute layers of wood with which to build its nest, all of these things and more can not only attract but also hold our attention for some time, with no thought of anything else. Better still, this entertainment is entirely free, available 24 hours a day, seven days a week, and we need do nothing else but sit or stand and watch.

If you have space, create a dedicated spot from which you can see the wildlife, but where they are less able to see you. This might be a chair just outside the back door, or under an arbour. Keep a reasonable distance from any bird feeders so that the birds are not put off by your presence, although the more time you spend out in the garden the more familiar with you they will become. (It is also nice to be able to see a bird feeder or bird bath from inside the house for a chance at a mindful moment when you are waiting for the kettle to boil.)

Bees, butterflies and other insects are less flighty, and all it takes is getting close to the flowers to see them. If you are less able to get down to the ground, consider a bench with integrated planters at either end, or placing a bench among a collection of large pots. When planted with plenty of flowers to attract wildlife, you will be able to see them at close quarters.

Having a diverse collection of wildlife that calls your garden home, or at least visits regularly, is not just of benefit to you as an interested observer, but also as a gardener. The greater the diversity, the more likely it is that there will be something in your garden that predates on pests, and no one problem can get out of hand. Birds, ladybirds and hoverflies (in particular the young larvae) all eat aphids in abundance. Slugs are a favourite of toads and hedgehogs (in the UK), and snails will be eaten by larger birds. Having a natural pest-control system reduces the need, and desire, to use chemical controls, especially as many of these can be harmful to the beneficial wildlife as well as the pests. You are also able to harvest your fruit and vegetable crops, and relish your flowers developing interesting seed pods, because of the pollinating services of visiting bees and other insects.

A cabbage white butterfly flitting on the breeze is a lovely sight. A cabbage white butterfly on your cabbages is not. Put up whatever barriers or deterrents you need to in order to preserve your crops to a harvest-level you are happy with, but remember that in order to maintain a healthy ecosystem of predators and prey (that is, a diverse collection of wildlife) in your garden it is necessary to tolerate a little damage to your plants.

Planting trees, shrubs, perennials and annuals that are especially valuable and attractive to wildlife is one way to bring them to your garden (see *Planting for birds*, *Planting for bees* and *Planting for butterflies and moths*, on pages 112, 113 and 114). However, there are a number of other measures you can take to help wildlife make a home there too (see overleaf).

Be mindful of wildlife

 Avoid using pesticides and other chemical sprays wherever possible, but especially on flowering plants. Slug pellets (and the slugs that have ingested them) will be poisonous to hedgehogs (in the UK) and amphibians, so do not use them.

 For birds, provide nesting boxes and a water source (e.g. a bird bath), as well as feeding stations stocked with nuts and seeds in the sparser, colder months (not just in winter but also in cold springs when there will be fewer bugs to eat and adults will be feeding their young). Feed according to the weather and not the time of year. Leave plants with seedheads standing over winter so that the birds can help themselves to the seeds.

 Provide nesting sites for solitary bees – old bamboo canes or proprietary purpose-built boxes are suitable for this. Bees rely heavily on the sun for energy, so plant bee-food plants in the sunniest spots, and in large clumps to make it easier for the bees to get from one to the other (as opposed to scattering such plants around the garden).

 Leave some fallen fruit under the tree as a food source for butterflies and other wildlife.

 Put up bat boxes in the garden or, if it is safe to do so, leave old hollow trees standing for them to nest in.

 Bats will not eat the plants themselves, but feed on the insects that are attracted to the garden. Pale and white-coloured plants attract more moths and night-time pollinators than darker-coloured plants, so include some of these as potential bat food.

 Leave a corner or patch of the garden untended and untidied for beetles and other insects to make their homes. Likewise, leaving the stems of herbaceous perennials standing over winter provides seasonal homes for many insects – just cut them back in early spring before the new growth pushes through. Many garden weeds (such as nettles/*Urtica dioica*, docks/*Rumex* and thistles/*Carduus*) are used by butterflies and moths as a place to lay their eggs. Thus, by providing a home for caterpillars, we get to see the butterflies.

Have an open compost heap, which will be home to many more species, such as slowworms, than a closed plastic bin, and the insects above it are a feast for bats. Avoid adding food scraps so as not to attract rats.

 Leave piles of leaves and old branches for hedgehogs (in the UK), and always restack and check bonfires before you light them.

 Create a wildlife corridor through your garden by making a small hole (for example, in the base of the fence) on each boundary. This is especially useful for allowing hedgehogs to come and go. Alternatively, dispense with the fence and plant a native hedge, with a mix of species (readily available from nursery retailers) that will provide berries, nuts and shelter for many animals, birds and insects.

 Adding a water source will attract a wide range of wildlife to your garden (see *Water in the mindful garden*, on pages 116–120).

 See *Further resources*, on pages 218–19, for sources of more information on attracting and caring for wildlife in your garden.

The plants listed on the following pages (see pages 112–114) are those that are suitable for a garden setting. Some "wildlife gardens" would include many other species, but these can also be considered weeds, especially in a small garden (for example, brambles/*Rubus fruticosus*). Other garden plants that are good for wildlife can be considered invasive on a wider scale: for example, in the UK the Royal Society for the Protection of Birds (RSPB) now advises against planting the butterfly bush (*Buddleja davidii*) because its small seeds spread far and wide so readily. Butterfly bushes also colonize and crowd out other plant species in habitats such as chalk grassland, which are home to rare invertebrates. On balance, the butterflies are able to find food on other plants, but the invertebrates cannot source anywhere else to live, so the butterfly bush is classed as invasive.

Planting for birds

Key:

(B) = berry and fruit plants
(N) = nesting and shelter plants
(S) = seed and nut plants

Alnus glutinosa (common alder) (S)

Berberis (barberry) (B, N)

Betula pendula (silver birch) (S)

Cornus mas (Cornelian cherry), *C. sanguinea* (common dogwood) (B)

Cotoneaster (B)

Crataegus monogyna (common hawthorn) (B, N)

Daphne mezereum (mezereon) (B)

Dipsacus fullonum (common teasel) (S)

Euonymus alatus (winged spindle tree) (B, N)

Left to right: *Alnus glutinosa* (common alder); blackbird (*Turdus merula*) with rosehips; *Pulmonaria officinalis* (common lungwort); *Colchicum autumnale* (meadow saffron)

Hedera helix (English ivy) (B, N)

Helianthus annuus (sunflower) (S)

Ilex aquifolium (English holly) (B, N)

Knautia arvensis (field scabious) (S)

Ligustrum ovalifolium (privet) (B, N)

Lonicera periclymenum (honeysuckle) (B, N)

Mahonia (Oregon grape) (B)

Malus (crab apple) (B)

Photinia davidiana (stranvaesia) (B)

Prumus. avium (wild cherry) (B, N)

Pyracantha (firethorn) (B)

Rosa canina (dog rose), *R. moyesii* (rose), *R. rugosa* (hedgerow rose) (B)

Sambucus nigra and cvs (common elder) (B, N)

Sorbus aria (whitebeam), *S. aucuparia* (rowan) (B, N)

Succisa pratensis (devil's bit scabious) (S)

Taxus baccata (yew) (B)

Viburnum betulifolium; *V. lantana* (wayfaring tree); *V. opulus* (guelder rose) (B)

Planting for bees

Bees will enjoy the nectar from many flowers – this is just a selection of the best choices. In general, opt for single open flowers rather than double ones, which have so many petals that the bees often cannot reach the nectar in the centre.

Ajuga reptans (bugle)
Aquilegia vulgaris (granny's bonnets)
Borago officinalis (borage)
Calamintha nepeta (lesser calamint)
Chaenomeles (flowering quince)
Colchicum (autumn crocus)
Cosmos bipinnatus (cosmea)
Crocus
Digitalis (foxglove)
Dahlia (single-flowered varieties)
Echinops (globe thistle)
Eryngium (sea holly)
Erysimum 'Bowles's Mauve' (wallflower)
Fuchsia

Geranium (cranesbill)
Helenium (sneezeweed)
Lavandula angustifolia (English lavender)
Lonicera × purpusii (Purpus honeysuckle)
Mentha (mint)
Nepeta cataria (catmint)
Primula veris (cowslip), *P. vulgaris* (primrose)
Prunus spp. (cherry/plum)
Pulmonaria officinalis (common lungwort)
Salvia (sage)
Sarcococca confusa (Christmas box)
Symphyotrichum
Tropaeolum majus (nasturtium)
Viburnum tinus (laurustinus)

Planting for butterflies and moths

The plants listed below will all supply butterflies and moths with nectar. Open, flat-topped (umbelliferous) plants will also be a good choice, as they supply not only the nectar but also a landing pad for the insects. Many of the plants on the bee list (see *Planting for bees*, on page 113) are also food plants for butterflies.

Achillea (yarrow)
Actaea simplex (baneberry)
Astrantia major (greater masterwort)
Aurinia saxatilis (gold basket)
Bergenia (elephant's ears)
Buddleja alternifolia (butterfly bush),
    B. globosa (orange ball tree)
Calluna (heather)

Caryopteris × *clandonensis*
Centaurea (knapweed)
Centranthus ruber (red valerian)
Cynara cardunculus (globe artichoke)
Dianthus barbatus (sweet William)
Erica (heather)
Erysimum cheiri (wallflower)
Heliotropium (heliotrope)
Hesperis matronalis (sweet rocket)
Matthiola incana (Brompton stock)
Nicotiana alata (flowering tobacco)
Prunus laurocerasus (cherry laurel)
Scabiosa (scabious)
Sedum (stonecrop)
Solidago (golden rod)
Spiraea japonica (Japanese spiraea)
Tagetes erecta (African marigold)
Verbena bonariensis (Argentinian vervain),
    V. hastata (American blue version)
Zinnia elegans

Left to right: *Zinnia elegans*; *Astrantia major* (greater masterwort); Queen of Spain fritillary butterfly (*Issoria lathonia*) on *Scabiosa* (scabious)

Water in the mindful garden

There is no doubt that water is a restful presence in the garden. Many people find the sound of moving water relaxing, and it can be a good source of white noise too (see *Sound*, on page 90). Water's reflective properties add a different quality of light to the garden, and there is always something to see on a pond, no matter how small. It could be the light rippling over the surface, water boatmen (*Corixa punctata*), a fish gliding lazily up to catch a fallen fly, a tadpole hatching from frogspawn or a waterlily (*Nymphaea*) flower bobbing quietly. Water encourages us to be quiet and observant – it encourages us to be mindful.

Philosophically, water in the garden reminds us of our connection with the world around us: how we are mostly made of water, as is everything else, and that water is constantly cycling around the world (and has been for millions of years). Thinking about how old the water we are looking at might be is a humbling experience. Spending some time looking at water, or listening to water moving – a small fountain perhaps – gives a clarity to our mind to equal that of the water.

Including a water feature in our gardens is also incredibly beneficial for wildlife. Birds and insects can drink from it and it will also attract and provide a home for specific water insects and amphibians such as frogs, toads and newts. All these creatures enhance the ecosystem in the garden – helping to keep pests in check. Amphibians, in particular, are excellent at clearing up slugs from the borders.

Even the smallest gardens can incorporate some kind of water. Not everyone has space for a large pond, but just a bird bath can be a worthwhile addition. Ponds also need not be large – if there is space for a bucket, there is room for a pond. There are even miniature pond plants suitable for such small containers. It is also not necessary to dig a hole, because raised ponds can be built on patios and other hard (or soft) surfaces. These can also incorporate seating and planted beds around them, making it much easier to get close to the Nature in the pond.

WHAT TYPE OF POND?

A pond can be made from any container that holds water. Ideally it should be at least 20–30cm (8–12in) deep so you can also include some pond plants and so that in hot weather there is still sufficient cool water at the base for the small water creatures. A pond of varying depths of 20–60cm (8–24in) will suit most pond life and plants

Decide whether you want to include a fountain. These can pump the water at a low bubble or in a high spray, and help oxygenate the water as well as adding visual and auditory interest. Again, fountains are available in a range of sizes for most ponds.

In a large garden, you could also consider adding a stream or rill component, and/or an adjacent bog garden to create more planting and habitat opportunities.

IN AND AROUND THE POND

Pond plants fall into three main groups and it is good to include representation from all of them if possible: oxygenators (usually submerged, free-floating); floating aquatic plants (such as waterlilies/*Nymphaea*, which should cover around two-thirds of the pond's surface); and marginal plants. The marginals need to be placed on shelves or the pond's base at the correct depth for their species so that the foliage protrudes from the water but the roots are below, in special planters of aquatic compost. Plenty of plants not only add interest for the gardener, but also for the wildlife, again introducing a range of habitats.

It is crucial to provide a means for animals and birds to get out of, as well as into, the pond because wildlife will be attracted to a pond whether we want it to be or not. It is even possible for amphibians to drown in a steep-sided,

slippery pond, so put in a ramp or stepped stones (preferably with a textured surface to give the creatures some purchase), to help them get to the side and out over the top.

Partial shade over a pond can be helpful for keeping algae under control, but ponds still need to be sited in some sun. Overhanging trees that shed their leaves in the pond can create a lot of work when clearing them out every autumn (stretching netting over the surface can help here).

Ponds can be lined with puddled clay or butyl or plastic liners, which can then be disguised with stones that offer hiding places for small pond fauna and rooting opportunities for plants.

To get as many mindful moments out of your pond as possible, put some seating close by so you can sit and watch the surface, or position your pond near a window so you can see the goings-on from the house. If it is big enough, you could even erect decking over some of the surface so that you can really look into the water.

See *Further resources*, on pages 218–19, for sources of more information on creating ponds.

Previous page: Raised ponds can be included in borders – here with a cool-coloured planting scheme of *Agapanthus, Verbena, Lupinus, Pennisetum* and *Salvia*

The balcony and indoor mindful gardens

Lack of outdoor space need not be a hindrance to mindful gardening. Indeed, plants in pots can require even more nurture and care than those growing in the open ground, because you are their only source of water, nutrients and light. Furthermore, having a plant at such close quarters – on your desk perhaps, or the kitchen windowsill – means that the plants are much more part of your life than if you were only out in the garden once or twice a day. You are able to take a few minutes to look at them, and give your mind a rest, whenever you like (so it is worth having a plant or cut flowers around you when indoors, even if you have a large garden).

Surrounding ourselves with greenery, especially in otherwise stale, lifeless environments such as many offices, has been shown to be beneficial to our health and productivity. Growing indoors also allows gardeners in temperate climates to grow plants that would not survive outside. Experimenting with growing exotic crops feeds our curiosity. When we try growing something just to see if it will grow – such as a mango from the seed in our fruit – it again rekindles some of the childlike enthusiasm we may have lost. We are also able to get really close to the plants – often closer than we could outside in a border – to really see, feel and smell them.

BALCONIES AND WINDOWSILLS

Balcony and windowsill gardens work just like any other container garden, though sites that are significantly elevated are prone to strong and drying winds. Plants in pots need regular watering and the application of fertilizer to provide nutrients, because the nutrients in the potting compost will be quickly exhausted by the plant. Almost any plant can be grown in a pot, providing the pot is large enough, so even without any soil it is possible to create a beautiful garden that stimulates the senses.

Herbs such as mint, sage, rosemary, oregano and thyme can all be grown in pots on a windowsill

Options for particularly sensory plants that would fit on a windowsill include all the major culinary herbs, such as sweet basil (*Ocimum basilicum*), parsley (*Petroselinum crispum*) and coriander/cilantro (*Coriandrum sativum*). Rosemary (*Rosmarinus*) and thyme (*Thymus*) can also be kept small with regular cutting to use in the kitchen, or try growing lemon grass (*Cymbopogon citratus*) or lemon verbena (*Aloysia citrodora*) for their wonderful citrus leaves. Other plants with scented leaves include the fragrant pelargoniums (often known as scented geraniums). These are available in aromas from citrus to rose and cinnamon and many more. Chilli pepper plants and tomato plants (e.g. 'Red Robin', plus other miniature varieties specifically bred for windowsill pots) provide wonderful tastes and perfumes as well as the sight of ripening fruits.

Indoor plants

Plants for indoors have both limitations and opportunities. Plants inside will get considerably less light than those outdoors, even if they are on a sunny windowsill; yet they can be kept at much higher temperatures. This is why many of the most successful indoor plants have their origins in the lower strata of tropical forests – hot but shady places. The only other consideration is humidity. Centrally heated houses tend to have very low humidity levels, and these can desiccate some plants. Therefore mist them with water if necessary, and avoid placing containerized plants near radiators.

Visiting specialist nurseries, flower shows and plant fairs will provide more choice of house plants than a garden centre, or try ordering online or asking friends for cuttings. Whatever our plants, we must always be mindful of their needs and nurture them, and in return they will give interest and pleasure, often for many years.

Small ornamental indoor plants might include orchids, whose textural leaves and delicate flowers are fascinating to look at in all their detail. The delta maidenhair fern (*Adiantum raddianum*) is often used just as a filler plant around flowering varieties, yet it is beautiful in its own right, with black stems holding almost impossibly thin leaves that flutter in the slightest breeze. African violets (*Saintpaulia*) are among the most compact of indoor plants, and Cape primrose (*Streptocarpus*) also has textured hairy leaves and delicate flowers.

The indoor gardener can also grow bulbs. Just store them in the refrigerator to mimic the cold winter spell they would experience outside, then plant them in pots of compost or rest them on a layer of stones in a vase so that the roots and shoots can also be seen as they develop. Tulips work well for this, as do hyacinths (*Hyacinthus*) and indoor daffodils such as the paper-white daffodil (*Narcissus papyraceus*). Cacti and other succulents are often overlooked as indoor plants, their slow-growing habit and lack of flowers being considered a bit dull. However, they are relatively low maintenance and, if you get up close, there is still plenty to see in their textured form and colour variations.

If you have more space – for a large pot or two on the floor, for example, in a conservatory or room with large windows – many of the larger indoor plants are also good for attracting the attention. Some of these can get quite large, but they are slow-growing and they will not get out of hand too quickly because they are being grown in a pot rather than the open ground. Abutilons have nodding, bell-shaped flowers in a range of colours, while the crimson bottlebrush, *Callistemon citrinus* 'Splendens', has fantastic red fragrant flowers that look just like a bottlebrush. Cape jasmine (*Gardenia jasminoides*) is well-known for its scent, but the dark glossy foliage is attractive too, as is that of the Swiss cheese plant (*Monstera deliciosa*). Kahili ginger (*Hedychium gardnerianum*) has tall spikes of foliage and fragrant flowers coming from the base. Small trees suitable for indoors include some fig (*Ficus*) species and citrus trees.

Growing a range of house plants will ensure you always have something to look at, smell or touch in your indoor garden. However, if you are hankering after a little more, cut flowers can help ring the seasonal changes. Buying locally grown ones (rather than year-round imports from the other side of the world) keeps you much more in tune with the seasons, and also gives you a wider choice. Locally grown blooms will have much more of a feel of the garden about them too, so even if you cannot grow them yourself you can still enjoy their beauty.

Indoor gardening is really no different to that outdoors when it comes to doing it mindfully. There are more distractions indoors – things you should be getting on with, such as the washing up or the ironing – but try to keep your attention focused on the plants and what you are doing. For example, watering pots requires concentration, because if they overflow that is water all over the windowsill and carpet. The water must be applied slowly, with plenty of pauses as you watch it sink in and wait to see it appear in the drip tray or saucer below. Incorporate some deep breaths to ground yourself before you start (see *Pausing on the threshold*, on pages 55–57). You will soon discover that you can gain just as much mindful benefit from gardening indoors as out.

CHAPTER 4

Mindful garden practice

Snobbery abounds when it comes to garden design, colour schemes and even to particular plants – one only has to look at how many plants, roses in particular, are given aristocratic or royal names. Some gardeners believe that the new (genetic) advances in breeding that give us dwarf sunflowers (*Helianthus*) and near-blue roses just should not be allowed; others think using plants with particular colours is gaudy, brash or garish. Ignore them all. Your garden is your space to create whatever you like – and that is the key. It is what you like and what has meaning for you. If you are going to be more mindful of your garden and look more closely more often, when you look it should make you happy. Imagine giving a tour of your garden to friends, or even strangers. How would you tell the story of your garden?

Spring

As spring awakens our plants, we too return to the garden refreshed and keen to get going after the winter break. Spring can seem to take a long time to get going some years, and it is very easy to become impatient for more growth after the initial crocus and daffodils (*Narcissus*) have had their say, but each day a little more light and a little more warmth creep into the garden. Even if we cannot detect these minute changes day to day, our plants can, and they will be busy below ground (if not above it), seeking out water and minerals ready to shoot forth as soon as the perfect time arrives.

It is said that spring moves at around 3km/h (2mph), so in theory we could walk alongside it. Whatever your personal marker of the arrival of spring, be it the first leaf on hawthorn (*Crataegus*) or the first sighting of a migrant bird, the season's inexorable progress brings new energy to the garden, and to us. We can feel that we start anew in the garden – we are as fresh as the air and new growth around us. Take some time to stand or sit and enjoy this feeling – the warmth of the sun and the air on your skin, the glistening dew on the plants early in the morning and the singing of the birds.

With all this new growth and excitement in the garden, it is wise to temper the situation a little – remember not to let the pleasant tip over the scale into the unpleasant by creating too much work for yourself further down the line (see pages 44–45). Heed the advice of 19th-century writer Henry Ward Beecher not to be "made wild by pompous catalogues from florists and seedsmen"!

The etymology of the month names are particularly interesting for spring time as in the northern hemisphere they pertain more to the natural world than any other season. March derives from Mars, the god. Commonly thought to be the god of war, he actually had a second role as the god or guardian of agriculture and wind. The March winds blow away all the

"All my life through, the new sights of Nature made me rejoice as if I were a child."

Marie Curie,
SCIENTIST

cobwebs of winter to allow us to start afresh. April is from the Latin *aperire* meaning "to open" or "to uncover", highly appropriate for the month in which many plants begin to put on their new shoots. May probably derives from the Roman earth god, Maia, who oversaw the growth of plants, for it is in this month that the first flushes of growth start to reach up and out in earnest. We too should oversee this growth and care for the tender shoots, and enjoy them in all their vivid and verdant glory.

PLANTING

Spring is an ideal time to plant: the soil is warming up (would you like your feet to be plunged into cold, hard ground?) and there is enough rain to keep it moist, so we are not called on too much to water. If we took the time to view our borders or pots critically last year, we will know which spots need something brighter, taller, shorter or more subtle; where there are gaps, and what needs splitting into smaller clumps; what did well in its position and what did not. Such a review is a good way to keep developing the garden, to keep reaching for perfection. All the best gardens are created through trial and error – we just have to have the confidence to pull out and replace a plant that is not doing what it should.

Preparation is key, so that the planting is not interrupted more often than it need be. Therefore, before you start planting, make sure you have everything you will need to hand, then ground yourself (see *Pausing on the threshold*, on pages 55–57). If your soil has not already been well prepared so that it is easy to dig, focus on the digging rhythm to bring you into a more mindful state.

Digging, whether it be with a trowel or a spade, is much easier to do when you can maintain a good momentum, a good rhythm. This can work well as an anchor for the mind, as it gives a steady beat to focus on. However, because it does not require all your attention, you can also have a broader awareness through your other senses. If the mind wanders away, bring it back first to the digging, then allow the other sights, sounds and smells to come in. Use

"More grows in the garden than the gardener sows."

Spanish proverb

the action of digging to create an up-and-down beat – rather like the left and right steps in walking – of the spade going into the soil and coming back out again. It does not matter how fast or slow you go, just try to keep it steady, and bring your attention to bear on the action. Feel the muscles you are using in your body for each movement, then bring the focus purely onto your arms as they tense and relax with each spadeful lifted.

The digging action will obviously be interrupted with each plant going into the ground, but by bringing the focus back to it each time you pick up the spade you are anchoring to the present. In your broader awareness you might:

See

the plants as they go into the ground, their fresh green growth and delicate leaves and stems, flower buds and new shoots; their pale roots waiting to explore their new home; the soil, its different shades and how it falls from the spade as you move it first from the hole and then back around the roots; the worms, bugs and beetles in the soil; and a bird hopping in for a quick snack.

Hear

the spade slicing into the soil, a clunk as it hits a stone; the muffled thud of soil falling off the trowel; loose soil falling onto the ground as you tip up the potted plant; the plastic tap of the empty pot as you put it down; and the birdsong, traffic or people in the wider environment.

Feel

the changing weight of the spade as you dig up and drop the soil; the damp rootball and soil in your hands; the pressure as you press down the soil around the rootball; and the stems and leaves brushing against your arms and legs.

Smell

the damp earth; sweet compost; and the leaves and flowers of the plant and of those around you.

Continue planting mindfully for as long as you want to: you might initially want to do this for just one plant going into the ground. Then try maintaining mindfulness for two plants next time. The more you practise, the easier it becomes.

Once you have finished planting and watering everything in (see *Watering*, on pages 142–43), step back and admire your work. Take a moment to consider the potential in what you have just done – how the plants will grow and expand and the pleasure they will bring in the seasons and years to come.

Sowing

There is a reason why gardeners who raise plants commercially do so in "nurseries" – bringing up a plant is much like raising a child. We care for them, nurture them, give them everything they need (but perhaps not everything they want) and do our best for them so that they can grow to their best potential. Raising plants from division, bulbs or cuttings is satisfying, but nothing beats the fulfilment of growing something from seed.

Seeds are the ultimate in humble potential. Their unassuming exterior conceals a storehouse of exactly what each needs to get out of the ground: an energy supply, and a tiny root and shoot. They do much more for us than we perhaps realize: for example, we would not be able to benefit from eating bread were it not for the energy in the wheat seed. As gardeners, we are required to give that seed only what it needs in order for it to burst into life – namely, water and the right levels of heat and darkness. Gardeners are rather like horticultural midwives in this respect: we bring the plant into the world, even though we had no hand in actually creating it.

Just like planting (see pages 130–33), the act of sowing seed can be wonderfully rhythmic and a brilliant opportunity to practise mindfulness. This applies whether we are sowing outside or in a greenhouse (or on a windowsill), in stations (spaced intervals) or drills (a thin continuous line), in the ground or in pots and trays. The more confident we get in using mindfulness, the more we can apply it to all our gardening activities, but start with a quick activity such as the actual seed-sowing itself. Each little sowing will act as a mini-mindfulness moment in itself.

There are no specific suggestions as to what to look, listen and feel for in this exercise, as the aim is to concentrate more fully on the rhythm of the sowing action for the short time you are maintaining it. However, you should try to keep that alert awareness as you move from one batch of seeds to the next.

As with all mindful gardening, the closer you can get to the soil and the less you use tools, the better. A dibber is a good tool for sowing seeds in stations, and for pots and trays, but you have four perfectly good dibbers on each hand so you do not need to buy one. You might get a little dirt under your fingernails, but you will also enjoy far more sensory stimulation which will help anchor you in the present.

Before you start sowing, make sure you have everything you will need to hand: the seeds, a full watering can, pots and trays filled with potting compost (if applicable), labels and a pencil. Rake the soil to a fine tilth or fill your pots and trays with compost. Also water the soil or compost in the pots/trays. Then ground yourself (see *Pausing on the threshold*, on pages 55–57).

For small seeds mark a drill in the soil or in the compost in the seed tray. Pour the seeds into your hand. Tap the seeds out of your hand by creating a funnel with your palm and tapping just above it with the other hand to shake the seeds out slowly. Do this with a steady rhythm and focus entirely on that beat, the feeling of the impact of each tap, the change in the shadows on your seed-holding hand as the other comes closer and further away, the falling of the seeds into the soil/compost. For sowing in pots or in stations, the rhythm is created by the alternate motions of creating the hole with the dibber (or finger) and putting in the seed.

Covering the seeds over is best done all at once at the end of the exercise. As you brush the soil back over the top of each station or drill, concentrate on the feeling of the soil on your fingertips. (Very fine seeds can be sprinkled directly onto the soil/compost surface and there is no need to cover them.) Make sure all your containers or drills are labelled with the plant name and sowing date, then take a moment to admire your work. A shelf of sown seeds is a powerhouse of potential, a garden in the offing. Now all you have to do is wait.

Summer

Summer is the time when our plantings of autumn and spring make their impact, a time for enjoying our gardens in the long days and (hopefully) warm sunshine. Now is not the time to be thinking too much of how we would improve things; instead it is an opportunity to put our feet up in that deckchair and listen to the birds singing and the bees buzzing. Every day brings something new to see – a flower that has opened, a young shoot, fruit that has ripened.

Of course there are still jobs to be done, namely watering (see pages 142–43), weeding (see pages 147–48) and, if you have a lawn, mowing (see pages 138–41), but these can be undertaken joyfully. There is pleasure to be found in every season, and the changes between them, but it is perhaps foolish to suggest that weeding boggy, claggy soil on a cold or wet winter's day is as nice as pulling up a weed on a balmy summer's evening.

Deadheading is another opportunity to practise mindfulness: use the rhythm of cutting each spent flower to anchor you in the present, with a wider awareness of the scent of the flowers, the feel of their foliage against your arms as you reach into the bed, as well as the texture of the stems and old flowers in your hands and the squeezing of your secateurs (hand pruners), scissors, snips or fingers.

It is good to take a little time to perform a review of the garden in summer. A quick walk round with a notebook or camera once a month to jot down where there are gaps or plants that need attention come autumn and spring will save a lot of head scratching later on. Nothing stands still, least of all plants, and a regular assessment of what is going well and what is not makes for a better garden year on year. (Performing this exercise in our wider lives has a lot of benefits too.)

MOWING

Fresh-cut grass is one of the defining smells of summer, and a lush green sward can set off the rest of the garden beautifully. Few can resist a lawn as a space for games and lounging, and it is a perk of the season to be able to spread out a rug for a picnic or for a place on which to enjoy a book. Well-cut lawns invite us to get closer too, to run our hand through the blades, or pat their tops to feel the springiness.

A lawn is, however, where we assert our dominance over Nature the most. That cut every week or two is constantly denying grass its opportunity to flower and set seed. If you are inclined to allow Nature a little more free rein, you might consider a flowering lawn or even a wildflower meadow in your garden. However, even these can benefit from a mown path through them – the juxtaposition of short and long grass improves the effect of both – so, whatever kind of lawn you have, some mowing is going to be necessary.

The introduction of noisy machinery to the situation does not chime with the normal application of mindfulness to gardening. However, although the lawnmower might exclude the possibility of being aware of sounds such as birdsong around you, it is still possible to mow the lawn in a mindful way. The steady pace up and down the grass is ideal for keeping the focus on that present task. If you think it might be dangerous to be mindful and use machinery at the same time, ask yourself whether it is better to be alert and fully aware of your surroundings or daydreaming while mowing.

Having got the lawnmower set up and then started, you should ground yourself (see *Pausing on the threshold*, on pages 55–57) before beginning to cut the grass. If you can do this in a regular, up-and-down-strips manner that is preferable, but obviously it depends entirely on the shape of the lawn. In general, mowing all the way around the edge of the area twice and then going up and down over the middle will give the best effect and is the most efficient.

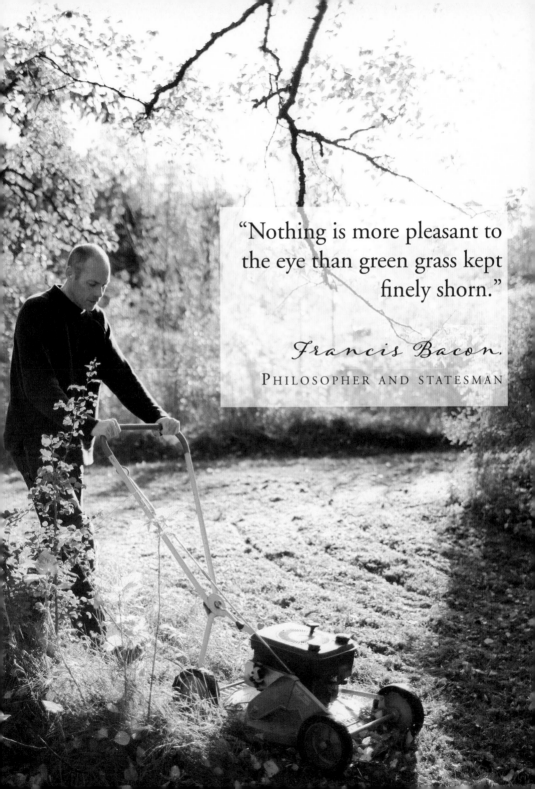

"Nothing is more pleasant to the eye than green grass kept finely shorn."

Francis Bacon.

PHILOSOPHER AND STATESMAN

You may find it helpful, for the first few sessions at least, to slow the mower speed down slightly, just until you are familiar with the mindfulness routine and how best to apply it when mowing your particular lawn. As you walk behind the lawnmower, bring your attention to the feeling of your feet lifting and then going back on the grass – the action of mindful walking (see pages 58–59). Maintain that focus on the pacing action, the rhythm of it, just lightly, to allow a broader awareness using the other senses.

Once you have finished cutting the grass, move the lawnmower safely out of the way, then get down onto the sward to take a closer look at your work. Run your hand over the grass, feeling the blades tickle its palm one by one. Look closely at the ends of each blade of grass – how does it look? Is it cut neatly, or is it torn? Torn grass will brown more easily at the ends and give a less tidy look to the overall lawn. To some extent the cut quality will depend on your type of lawnmower, but it may be worth looking at sharpening the blades.

Finish by cleaning the lawnmower and packing it away, then take another few mindful moments to stand and admire your work. The grass will grow again, potentially very quickly, but for now the lawn is perfect. Breathe deeply, savouring again the newly cut-grass smell. Look at the lawn itself and also how it fits with its surroundings – the plants that arch out of the bed over the grass, the tree that rises from the lawn, and the neat edges between grass and path.

See

the lawn with its shorter
grass and its uncut longer
parts; how the grass bends under
the mower; the small pieces of
cut grass – are they in clumps
or scattered? Clumps could
indicate a blockage or that
the grass is too damp
for mowing.

Smell

the herbaceous scent
of the fresh-cut grass and
the exhaust fumes of
petrol lawnmowers.

Feel

the vibrations of the
mower in your hands,
the contrast between the
different materials – metal
and plastic – and any
bumps on the handle.

WATERING

There are few tasks in the garden that better illustrate the interconnections of Nature than watering. We and all the plants around us are made up mostly of water – water that has been round and round the Earth perhaps billions of times.

There are lessons we can learn from water: namely that there is no obstacle too big. Water's first approach is to be flexible – it will divert and try to find another route. If it cannot go round an obstacle, or over it or under it, then like the family on Michael Rosen's *We're Going on a Bear Hunt* it will have to go through it. This might take many years, but water's persistence will ultimately wear away many metres of rock – witness the Grand Canyon – to find its best route back to the sea.

As a gardener, watering is both a humbling exercise in nurture (we are literally carrying the water to the plants and soil that need it) and a chance to use mindfulness to become a better gardener. Using mindfulness to observe our plants properly, as well as the soil or potting compost that they are growing in, ensures that we never over- or underwater our plants. We come to understand the needs of our plants and soil better, and how they change with the season and with the weather. For example, we might see a plant drooping horribly on a sunny day, assume (while our mind is on other things) that it is wilting through lack of water and rush out with the watering can. However, by taking a moment to look at the plant and the soil properly, we realize that the soil has plenty of moisture and the stem is actually relatively turgid; it is just the leaves that have flagged. This is not drought, it is sun-wilt – a temporary mechanism adopted by some plants in the midday heat to conserve water. Watering it now could mean the plant's roots drown in too much water, and the moisture that did evaporate would create a humid atmosphere around the plant, which could encourage fungal disease.

Watering is best carried out early in the morning or in the evening, when the applied water will evaporate least before it can get to the roots. These are also ideal times to incorporate some mindfulness, to balance the mind before beginning the rest of the day or going to sleep. Mindful watering can be done using a watering can or a garden hose – the point of this exercise is to pay attention to the water as it goes into the soil or container.

As always, make sure you have everything needed to hand and that distractions such as the radio or your phone have been turned off, then ground yourself (see *Pausing on the threshold*, on pages 55–57). This guidance refers to the action of applying water to the soil or compost; if it is also necessary to walk to and from a tap, try to do so using the tips for mindful walking (see pages 58–59). Water the garden methodically, working around it in one direction so that nothing gets missed; the plants may not all need watering, but they will all need checking.

Before watering each new part of the garden, look closely at its surface – does it look dry and dusty, wet and boggy, or somewhere in between? Push your finger into the soil/compost to assess the moisture level around the roots. Ideally, the soil should be moist, not soggy or dry (unless, of course, they are specialist plants, such as succulents), and a few particles should stick to your finger. Concentrate on feeling the soil on your fingers, trying to experience it directly rather than narrating to yourself what you are doing.

Where the soil or compost is dry, water thoroughly (an insufficient splash will only encourage the roots up to the surface where they will dry out faster). A good watering may mean pouring some water onto the soil and then letting it sink in before applying more, otherwise it simply runs off.

As you pour the water from the watering can or spray it from the garden hose, focus on the sense of sight. Look at the soil/compost as the water hits it – the dust that is thrown up by the impact, the changing colour as the water saturates the soil, the contrast between bright reflective water and dark soil. Notice as the soil becomes full of water and puddles on the surface; pause for a moment while it sinks in, then water again or else move on to the next plant as appropriate.

WEEDING

After pests and diseases, weeds are probably the issue that plagues gardeners most. They are impossible to get rid of, for even if we created an Eden-style biome over the garden and imported sterile soil we could still bring weed seeds in on shoes and clothing, so we have to admire their tenacity. In fact, "weeds" are a man-made concept in more ways than one. First, many of what we call weeds are wild flowers (often great for bees and butterflies) or even food crops such as dandelions (*Taraxacum officinale*), so subject to classification by the gardener. Secondly, many weeds do not exist in the wild and have adapted to grow exclusively in the cultivated soil of our gardens and farms, often evolving far faster and more effectively than any nurseryman could breed them. In literature and culture, weeds tend to be the bad guy, or the rebel, often romanticized as symbols of freedom (*the* weed, marijuana) and wilderness.

Mentally weeds are our bad thoughts, feelings we would rather we did not have. However, as in the garden, if it were not for us they would not be there. We must learn to accept that the bad thoughts are part of us, just as the weeds are part of the garden. Trying to ignore them will not make them go away (in fact, they will only get bigger), so we need to approach weeding with firm determination, but also a gentle attitude. Pulling at the weeds angrily will either scatter the seeds further around the garden or remove only the tops, allowing the roots to regenerate, and the weeds to multiply. If a patch of garden has become overrun with weeds, it can be a daunting prospect, and we can often wonder where to start. The longer we put off dealing with it, the worse the problem gets, and the scarier it becomes. Start somewhere small, and with time, patience and a little effort we soon create some space, and then a little more and a little more. This is how mindfulness works: by taking a moment to have a rest from our thoughts, over time we create space in our heads.

Weeding is literally cultivating the soil – we are bringing culture (i.e. our ethical and moral choices and consciousness) to bear on which plants we want to keep and which we would rather were not there. Try to avoid using war terminology when it comes to weeding (or indeed dealing with pests and diseases): weeds are just plants in the wrong place. All they want to do is flower and propagate themselves – they are not growing to spite us, and if we learn about them we can utilize some of their benefits as food sources, plants for wildlife or even medicine. Learning to identify weeds allows us to decide not only which ones it would be best to get rid of, but also how to remove them effectively. As with all gardening, the more we learn, the better we get.

Ground yourself (see *Pausing on the threshold*, on pages 55–57) before you start weeding, whether it be for a five-minute popping out into the garden or for a more dedicated session. Maintain the mindful awareness for as long as you like, but be sure to finish consciously, rather than letting your mind drift off and not reining it back, before deciding to stop.

See

the weeds, without imposing any construct on them. Observe their foliage – do they have wide or narrow leaves? What about the flowers – are they on spikes, in open cups, flat or nodding bells? What colour are they? As you dig up each weed, look at its roots – the long taproots of docks (*Rumex*), the fibrous mat of creeping buttercups (*Ranunculus repens*). See the flash of your hand fork as it moves in and out of the soil.

Hear

the soil falling from each weed's roots; the slicing of the fork into the ground; a ping as it hits a stone; and the thud as the weed falls into the bucket.

Feel

the weight of the weeds in one hand, the spikes from their defensive thorns and stings; and the weight of the fork and of the bucket as it fills.

Smell

the crushed foliage (many weeds have a distinctive scent); the hot or damp soil; and the flowers and plants around you.

Autumn

As summer comes to a close, flowers begin to fade and leaves start to fall. Although it can be sad to think that another growing season is over, there is still plenty to be enjoyed for its own sake – kicking through piles of leaves and the season's harvests. Autumn is also an ideal time to contemplate impermanence, an important theme in Buddhist doctrine. Death is not something to shy away from; it is all around us, every day, and if we regularly acknowledge impermanence it is not depressing, and in fact we learn to appreciate life all the more. When death does come, we are able to face it with greater equanimity and peace. Trying to hide from or deny impermanence gets harder the longer we try to do it, because we become ever more sensitive to changes in the status quo.

The season's activities in the garden all revolve around impermanence too: clearing leaves, composting and harvesting the last of our fruit and vegetables. Nature embodies impermanence; it is ever-changing. The seasons and years roll on from one to the next, inexorably and without apology: new flowers are always blooming; more fruit and vegetables are maturing; trees are growing up and out, then falling back to earth. By appreciating the present moment fully, we learn to value what we have right now, not what we used to have or would like to have in the future.

The history books teach us that time is linear, but spending time in the garden encourages a more cyclical view. Using time-lapse photography, nature documentaries are excellent at showing us leaves falling to the forest floor, rotting and being taken into the soil by worms, where their nutrients feed the roots and their bulk aerates the soil, so that the tree can burst into growth the following spring. The flowers on our dahlias are not gone forever; they will be back next summer, and the summer after that. The poppies (*Papaver*) that have lost their petals and set seed may die, but the seeds will bring them back as new plants next year; and the apples that have fallen from the tree now make room for more fruit to grow.

See

birds landing on seedheads; water droplets on cobwebs; leaves falling from trees; the final blossoms in the borders; the dew glistening on the grass; mushrooms and toadstools poking through the leaf litter; the branches and stems of trees and plants heavy with fruit; and the last of your vegetables hiding under yellowing foliage.

Smell

the crisp coldness of the air, its damp freshness; the putrid rotting of old cabbage leaves yet to be cleared from the vegetable patch; and the distinctive scent of each fruit, vegetable and flower.

Feel

the warmth of the sun on your face, or the drops of an autumn shower; the moisture brushing off the leaves onto your hand and arm; and the brittle old stems of plants as you move past them.

Hear

the crunch of your footfall across the garden; birds in the sky above, perhaps migrating, and others – closer – staking out territory for the winter; the soft thud of a falling apple; squirrels scampering through the treetops and along fences; and bees buzzing in the last of the flowers.

"Where are the songs of Spring? Ay, where
are they?
     Think not of them, thou hast thy music
too,—
   While barred clouds bloom the soft-dying day,
     And touch the stubble-plains with rosy hue;
Then in a wailful choir the small gnats mourn
     Among the river-sallows, borne aloft
          Or sinking as the light wind lives or dies;
   And full-grown lambs loud bleat from
hilly bourn;
     Hedge-crickets sing; and now with
treble soft
     The red breast whistles from a garden-croft;
          And gathering swallows twitter in
the skies."

John Keats,
ODE TO AUTUMN

Composting

Nowhere is the circle of life more apparent than in the compost heap. The more compost we make, the more obvious the cycle becomes, and the easier it is to see not only old flowers in the compost, but also the compost in new flowers. The constant revolution of growth and decay and more growth again can be a source not only of consolation but also of fresh hope. Those pumpkins might have succumbed to an unexpected frost, but their squishy flesh will be redeemed as beautiful compost with which to mulch the new pumpkin plants next summer. Likewise, triumphs such as this year's stunning sweet peas (*Lathyrus odoratus*) do not live forever, but will return in another form to help create more successes in the garden next year.

Although the death of the plants, or at least their top halves, might be the base ingredients of compost, the act of making it is undoubtedly positive. Compost, good compost, is created. If we were to simply chuck all our prunings, grass clippings and old foliage in a big pile in a dank corner of the garden, we would ultimately get something we could use on the beds, but it would take a long time and not be of the best quality – seams of stinking wet rot alternating with still-intact stems. We need to give the heap attention, turn and mix it, make sure that we do not put anything on it that might come back to haunt us (such as hedge bindweed/*Calystegia sepium* root or annual weed seeds), and have patience. Finally it will be ready, and we can put it back to work on the soil, imparting all its goodness to our plants once again.

Whether you make your compost in an enclosed bin or open bay, the guidance below is the same, as both benefit from regular turning. Use the repetitive motion of the turning action on which to anchor your focus, and allow that to engender a wider awareness of the garden around you. Revolving drum composters can still be used as a mindful exercise, but keep the focus on the movement of turning the drum, the sound of the compost falling over and over inside, and the change in light and shade on the surface of the drum.

Begin by gathering your tools and gloves together, standing in front of your task and taking a few deep breaths to ground yourself (see *Pausing on the threshold*, on pages 55–57). As you bend (remember to use your legs as well as your arms to get down to the compost, to save the strain on your back), feel the muscles you are using, the motion of scooping up a forkful of compost and turning it to the side, then returning to the pile for another scoop. At first, just be aware of your whole body moving, then turn your attention to just the legs. After a minute or two, focus on your arms, the tension and relaxation as they lift the weight of compost and then let it go for each scoop. Continue concentrating on the arms as you turn over the whole compost pile, but rest your attention only gently on the movement, just enough to bring your mind back every time it wanders. Allow the other senses to be aware of your surroundings, what you can see, hear and smell.

Smell

the compost itself. When it is fully rotted down and ready to use, it will smell sweet; areas that are not decomposing properly will smell mouldy, so use your nose as well as your eyes as a guide to ensure your heap is healthy. Also inhale the cold air and perhaps the smoke from distant bonfires.

See

the different ingredients of the compost in the overall pile: pieces of stalk and leaf, twig and flower, as well as the fauna of the compost heap – worms, beetles and more; any fungi blooming (break up and aerate these parts the most); the difference in colour between the seams of compost, and how the base of the pile has rotted more than the top; your breath on the cold air; and the steam rising from the compost.

Hear

the scoop and thud as you turn over each forkful or shovelful; the compost falling down the heap as it is disturbed; the creak of any plastic or wood as it moves; and birdsong, voices and traffic in the wider environment.

Harvesting

Autumn is when our patience with long-ripening crops is finally repaid. Pumpkins, brassicas and more have been in the ground for many months, and we have been protecting them in anticipation of this moment. The fruit trees we look after year-round are bearing apples, pears, quince and more.

Yet still we need patience. The beauty of home-grown produce is that it can be harvested when fully ripe (most grocery store items are picked unripe for ease of transport), so do not waste that opportunity by removing it too soon. Neither will grabbing at the fruit or vegetable do us or the plant any favours; we are more likely to break a branch or the intended harvest that way, or step on another plant in our haste. Be mindful of the plant and your actions to avoid any damage. Leaving a few items for the birds is a generous act.

Harvest is a time for celebration, not just of our crops, but also of the beauty in maturity. It is a lesson in ripening with grace, in not resisting our own aging. We are grateful for the ripening of the fruit, so we should not be ungrateful for the extra wrinkles on our faces. Mindfulness teaches us to appreciate what we have and where we are right now, not to be forever lamenting what is lost. The apple tree does not mourn the blossom it had produced earlier – it needed the flowers to develop the fruit. As we go about the garden, picking vegetables, fruit and the last of the autumn flowers, we should be grateful for each and every one of them. The apple harvest might not be as good this year as last, but it will still be delicious, so enjoy it for what it is.

Once you are out in the garden with your trug, basket or bag, pause for a moment to ground yourself (see *Pausing on the threshold*, on pages 55–57). It is almost possible to feel the season in the air in autumn, especially when you are about to enjoy its bounty. Keep a soft focus on the tread of your feet (see *Mindful walking*, on pages 58–59) and enjoy the maturity and decay in its full glory.

Feel

the movement in your body, your fingers closing around the flesh or stem each time you reach to pick a piece of fruit, vegetable or flower; the pressure you exert to remove it from the plant; and the weight of each fruit, vegetable or flower once off the parent plant.

Sense

the squeezing of your hand around the secateurs (hand pruners) or scissors as you cut any stalks.

Smell

the scent before putting the fruit, vegetable or flower in the basket and returning for another.

Taste

some of your harvest, because it is at its freshest and sweetest when straight off the plant.

See

the colours of each piece of fruit, vegetable or flower as you harvest.

See

the vivid colours of the leaves, the reds, yellows and oranges, and how the brown leaves serve only to highlight the colours even more; how the chlorophyll in an individual leaf has retreated to the central rib; how the leaves tumble and curl beneath the rake, and blow up and round in the breeze; and the different shapes and sizes of the leaves (which trees are shedding theirs now? Which are still holding on?).

Hear

the crunch of the leaves as you walk through them; the scratch of the rake and how it differs between grass, paving and gravel; and rustling from any leaves still on the trees.

Feel

the smooth handle of the rake in your hands; the contrast between the cold air and your warm skin; the vibration of the rake as it jumps over bumpy patches, and the weight of the leaves you are pulling with it; and the damp or dry leaves, their softness compared with the rigid rake as you unclog the tines.

Smell

the fresh autumn air; the crushed leaves (some species have distinctive scents); and the mist and wood smoke.

Leaf clearing

Hues of gold and red, yellow and orange, the gentle rustling in the breeze…
trees really do make it easy for us to appreciate the wonders of the autumn
season. Of course, the vividness and length of the display varies from year to
year, depending on the weather conditions, but there is always some colour
to see, especially from certain tree species (see *Plants for sight*, on pages
80–81). Maples (*Acer*) are a good example, and why tourists flock to New
England and Japan to see their annual shows (a holiday known in some
parts as leaf-peeping).

But all that grows must die and all that rises must fall – and the leaves do
eventually drop. It is up to us as gardeners to clear them away. We do not
have to, we could leave them on the ground to rot in their own time as they
do in natural woodland, but to do so would mean the grass, and possibly
border plants, beneath would suffer from the lack of light and air. By clearing
away the leaves we also get the opportunity to make leafmould, a form of
compost made purely from leaves that is a wonderful addition to any soil.
Gardening is interference with Nature, but by replicating its methods (just in
a slightly tidier way) we minimize that interference.

Fallen leaves are another opportunity to rekindle our inner child. Who does
not love kicking up a pile of crispy, crunchy leaves? Or running through
them to find the shiniest conkers and fattest chestnuts? Catching the leaves as
they fall from the trees is a time-consuming way to clear them up, but a lot
of fun and something that requires complete focus on the present. There is a
superstition that to catch a leaf before it hits the ground is lucky: catch 12 –
one for each month – and you will be lucky for the following year.

Sweeping or raking up the autumn leaves is a job that needs patience, and
acceptance of forces outside our control.

On a still day it can be a therapeutic task. Raking or sweeping is far preferable to using a leaf blower, because it is much better exercise, uses no petrochemicals, and both your own focus on the world around and your neighbours' is not disturbed by the engine noise. With a rake you can be as one with your garden, while with a blower you are an intruder. Clearing away old leaves, making space in the garden again, can help the mind feel tidier too. Use it as an opportunity for mindfulness practice and you can return to the house refreshed and centred.

Ground yourself before starting (see *Pausing on the threshold*, on pages 55–57), then pick up your rake. Work methodically around the garden, as this will not only make the clearing up more efficient, but also help in maintaining your focus through the rhythm.

As you rake, start with an initial awareness of the whole body as it moves to bring the leaves closer and into a pile. After a minute or two, focus your attention only on your arms, on the stretching and pulling motion as you move the rake to gather the leaves. Keep this motion as steady as possible, as this is the rhythm that you will maintain your soft focus on for as long as you like, and the one that you can return to if your attention wanders. By harnessing your mind to the regular raking motion, you automatically have a wider awareness of the sensations around you.

Once you have your pile of leaves, end the mindfulness exercise. Now is the time to tidy them away into a bin or bags to create leafmould, or even have the chance to run through the pile for the pure joy of it.

Winter

Less is more, as the saying goes, and this is particularly true in the winter garden. Now is not the time for colourful flowers and lush growth; the eyes and the mind need a rest after the carnival of summer and autumn. Now is the time for simplicity, for a plain contrast of light and dark, of snow and hedge, or sky and tree. There is beauty in the starkness of the winter garden, the time when its bones are revealed to the world. Those evergreen shrubs and hedges and topiary, those upright bare trees, all show their strength by surviving through winter, but this is also their time to shine, for when there is nothing else to distract us we see their unpretentious beauty all the more clearly. The winter garden is quieter too, with no buzzing bees and fewer singing birds, less foliage to rustle and fewer people outside, so it is a perfect place to seek some peace.

Although there are still some jobs to be done in the garden, winter is the main season of rest for us as well as the plants. Nature needs the winter as much as the summer. It is a time to take stock, regroup and prepare for the business of the spring and summer ahead, but also a time to be still. For some, the shorter, darker, colder days are something to be endured (or escaped), yet getting out into the garden – even if it is just to walk – will bring a rosy glow to the heart as well as the cheeks. Winter will pass as surely as summer and autumn did before them, and with patience it will be spring again. In the meantime try to enjoy the opportunity to rest – and the seasonal beauty.

The main tasks at this time of year are pruning and, in early or late winter, some digging over if you are breaking new ground, perhaps for a new border or vegetable garden. On rainy days take shelter in the shed to clean and organize your tools, sort out seeds and have a good tidy, for come spring there will be less time for these jobs.

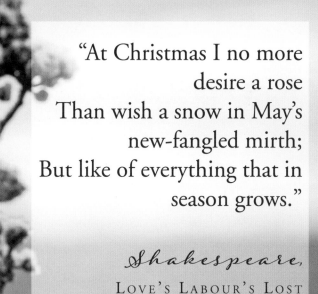

"At Christmas I no more
desire a rose
Than wish a snow in May's
new-fangled mirth;
But like of everything that in
season grows."

Shakespeare,
LOVE'S LABOUR'S LOST

PRUNING

Pruning is often a daunting prospect for a gardener, and the wealth of information about how and when to prune each species of shrub and tree can seem off-putting rather than helpful. One option is to attack everything, regardless of its flowering time and growth habit, using loppers and a hedge-trimmer, but this may well cause unsatisfactory results. Nor is leaving everything alone a good choice, if we do not want our backyards to return to woodland. Pruning – and being mindful of the method and effect – is the only answer.

All the pruning information and guidance boils down to a few key rules, and at the root of all of them is understanding why we are pruning each plant. Pruning is carried out to promote flowering or fruiting (for example, on a rose or apple tree, respectively), to maintain a healthy plant free from dead or diseased wood, and to create a good strong framework of branches that is aesthetically pleasing. Cutting off the tips of strong central branches leads plants to put on bushier growth. Understanding why we prune enables us to make that cut deliberate: a measured, mindful approach gives the best results for the plant and for the gardener.

Pruning is an excellent task for practising mindfulness because it requires total concentration and attention to the task to do it well. Think of the opposite attitude: trimming with a noisy machine typifies gardening on autopilot. There is a greater connection with the plant itself when using hand tools such as secateurs (hand pruners), loppers or a handsaw. Every cut is felt, and the effort that the gardener puts into making the incision means that each one is considered before it is done.

Pruning creates space for the plant to put on new and better growth. Allowing it to do this slowly, by trimming back new shoots a little every year, creates a stronger plant. It looks less, but it is actually more: more space and

See

the colour of the leaves and if they look healthy or patched with disease; spent flowers and their number; the framework of branches and whether it is open, allowing air to flow freely, or congested, with lots of small (perhaps dead) shoots in the centre; and whether the branches are showing any signs of disease or withering.

Smell

the freshly pruned wood; and the cold air.

Feel

the weight of your secateurs (hand pruners), loppers or saw in your hand, the smooth handle, the cold metal of the blade; the branches and leaves against your hands, arms, body and legs; dew brushing off onto your skin; the branch as you take hold of it, the rough or smooth bark; and the tension in your hand and arm as you make the cut.

Hear

the creaks of overladen or perhaps diseased branches; the breeze rustling the leaves – notice if it does not even penetrate the centre; and insects buzzing in the plant.

more energy. The same is true mentally – by removing branches of thought that are no longer helpful we create space in the mind for better things. We can, literally as well as metaphorically, see the wood for the trees.

With your tools at the ready, ground yourself (see *Pausing on the threshold*, on pages 55–57). Then look closely at the plant, its leaves (if it has any at the time of pruning), branches, stem or trunk and assess what needs to be taken out. Look at where you are going to make the first incision: find the healthy wood below the dead/diseased part and locate a healthy outward-facing bud to prune above. Be sure that this cut and removal will be helpful to the plant. Get in position to make the incision, feeling the movements as you make them, then slice or saw off the branch. Continue to remove the necessary branches, really looking, feeling and listening as you go. Any time you notice your attention has wandered, as it inevitably will, bring the focus back to the senses.

Finally, step back and appreciate your work and how it will benefit you, the plant and the rest of the garden.

DIGGING

As with all mindful gardening, aligning our interests with Nature and understanding how it works means that we can garden more efficiently and effectively. Digging itself, one of the most rhythmic tasks in the gardening calendar, is a perfect opportunity to practise mindfulness.

Digging used to be something that was done every winter, a man's job, and allotment sites and vegetable gardens were excavated to two spit's depth (a spit is the length of the spade blade) and refilled like clockwork. These days we understand more about the flora and fauna of the soil, and that has informed our treatment of it. The soil is an incredibly complex ecosystem, and no two areas are the same, but suffice it to say that there are a lot of creatures and fungi within the soil that do all the work of digging for us, if we would only let them. Digging serves only to disturb this delicate balance, and hinders the flora and fauna of the soil.

That said, there are still some situations in which digging is appropriate, in particular when breaking new ground, or in a compacted area that needs aeration. At such times digging allows for the incorporation of plenty of well-rotted garden compost or other organic matter to get the soil flora and fauna off to a good start again, and to break up areas of compaction for better drainage and root penetration. We can also remove any large stones and perennial weed roots at the same time, so that our plants have the best possible home when we come to put them in.

Begin by taking everything you will need – spade, garden fork, rake, a wheelbarrow full of garden compost (if applicable) – to the spot in the garden where you are digging. Rid the area of any distractions, such as radios or phones, and ground yourself with some deep breaths (see *Pausing on the threshold*, on pages 55–57).

Work methodically over the area, in rows up and down, to ensure that you can maintain a steady rhythm and that the whole area is covered. In this exercise, the subtle focus will be on the movement of the spade in and out of the soil, which will then allow and encourage a wider alert awareness of your surroundings. The main process of turning over the soil is a sufficiently long exercise, but if you are digging only a small space, or wish to carry on, apply the same methodology when adding any compost, forking it over, digging it in and, finally, raking the soil to a finer tilth. If you have clay soil, dig it only very roughly at first, allowing the soil to remain in large clods on the surface. Do this in early winter and leave it until late winter. By then the constant freezing and defrosting of the water between the soil particles will break them apart for you and you will be left with a lovely tilth that needs only minimal attention to get it plant-ready.

"We must cultivate our garden."
[*Il faut cultivar notre jardin*]

Voltaire,
PHILOSOPHER

As you start to dig, concentrate on how the body is moving, what muscles you are using in your arms, legs and torso. Feel the strain of lifting the laden spade, and the release of the soil sliding off, as well as the bend of the knees and elbows, and the step backward with each new spadeful. After a few minutes, focus attention on the leg that is driving the spade into the soil, and let that regular movement become the anchor for your mind. Should your attention wander, bring it back each time to the sensation of the muscles of your thigh pushing down on the spade. As you maintain focus on this, your mind will also become more attentive to the world around you.

See

the gleaming blade slicing through the soil; the shades of brown and black in the soil, the undulations, ridges and clumps; worms and other soil fauna; and your breath on the cold air.

Feel

the smooth shaft of the spade handle, and how it gets warmer the longer you use it; the rough texture of stones and cold foliage of weeds and roots as you remove them; and the changing weight of the spade depending on how much soil you have on the blade.

Hear

the ping of metal spade hitting stones; the singing of the bird that has arrived for a snack of whatever you turn up; and the muffled thud of soil hitting soil as you turn it over.

Smell

the biting air; the sweet compost; and the crushed foliage of weeds.

CHAPTER 5

Mindful garden projects

These nine projects are little self-contained mindfulness exercises. While the *Mindful garden practice* chapter (see pages 126–71) showed how to incorporate mindfulness into our everyday gardening tasks, these projects can be undertaken as a specific opportunity to get a little space in the mind and to take a break.

Each project also highlights a different feeling that we might want to focus on as we go through the exercise: gratitude (see *Contemplating gratitude*, on pages 214–15), for example, or generosity (see *Contemplating generosity*, on pages 194–95). Gratitude and appreciation in particular have been shown to significantly increase our levels of happiness by simply acknowledging for what we are grateful. A study in 2003 discovered that compared with writing down things that annoyed them or a simple recording of events, noting down three things that the participants were grateful for every day made them happier, more optimistic and physically healthier (they even exercised more!).

Positive attitude

By cultivating a confident outlook in ourselves, we create more positivity that comes back to us. Whether or not you believe in any religion, or life force (karma, chi or prana), being assured and having affirmative feelings are undoubtedly more beneficial than the reverse. By nurturing a plant we find that we have cared for ourselves as well; by giving away plants we create a feeling of abundance, not scarcity. Patience, curiosity, kindness and creativity are all emotions that are encouraged by being mindful, and by quieting the negative chatter in our minds we find that there is more space for these positive feelings. Try to approach these tasks with the sense of being a beginner, even if you are an experienced gardener. As a novice, we are naturally more curious – how does this work? why do we do that? – and life seems to be full of more possibilities than if we think we already know all the answers.

These exercises could last 10 minutes, an hour or more, or just a few minutes a day spread over several months. In each of them try to maintain the same alert awareness of your activities as when you cultivate the soil and plants. Keep the focus on your movements, and an automatic awareness of the world around you will follow.

It is not necessary to include the contemplations if you do not want to, but it can enhance the exercise. As with all mindfulness practice, begin each exercise by removing all distractions such as radios and phones, and start with some deep breaths to ground yourself (see *Pausing on the threshold*, on pages 55–57).

Growing tomatoes from seed

Annual plants – those that grow from a seed to flower, bear fruit and set seed again in a single year or growing season – are the ideal candidates for an exercise in nurture. We can raise a plant from infancy to maturity, caring for it every step of the way. To see it grow healthily is satisfying enough, but then to enjoy the flower and fruit is a huge reward for the effort we put in, and we can savour the fruit even more knowing that it fulfils precisely what the plant needs to happen.

"He who cultivates a garden, and brings to perfection flowers and fruits, cultivates and advances at the same time his own nature."

Ezra Weston,

GARDENER

Contemplating nurture

As you tend to your tomato plant, reflect on the care and attention that you are giving it. The plant spent all its energy on creating seeds so that they could go out into the world and become their own plants. Each seed had within it a first stem, leaves and roots that are now growing: all that it needed were the optimum conditions to unleash its potential. Nurture is about a constant attention to something's needs. You cannot bring something into life and then abandon it. Thus nurture is a process that requires commitment. As a plant grows, its requirements change, and you must provide it with the best you can for each stage of its life, even if that means taking something away. By growing a tomato plant, it provides you with tomatoes for food. What you nurture nurtures you.

1 In early spring gather together a pot, some seed or potting compost and a packet of tomato seeds. Then take a moment to ground yourself (see *Pausing on the threshold*, on pages 55–57).

2 Fill a small pot with potting compost, tapping it down on the work surface so that it settles and dislodges any air pockets, then water it thoroughly. Sprinkle the seeds thinly over the top of the compost, then cover with a thin layer of more compost. Put the pot in a warm place (at least 15°C/59°F, preferably nearer 20°C/68°F); a clear plastic bag over the top will help keep the temperature and humidity up.

3 Check the pot daily, and water if necessary to keep the compost moist. The seeds should germinate in 1–2 weeks.

4 Once shoots appear above the surface, remove the bag and move the pot to somewhere with as much light as possible (if it is not already), but that is still relatively warm and free from draughts. Watch as each bent shoot pushes up through the surface, then unfurls to become straight, pulling up the leaves and extending them into the light. Observe how the stem is initially white but soon turns green in the presence of light. Keep watering the pot as the compost needs it.

5 Soon the seedlings will develop their second set of leaves – the first "true" set. These are toothed and shaped more akin to a mature tomato leaf, unlike the seed leaves, which have smooth edges. Once the true leaves have developed it is time to move the strongest seedling(s) into their own pots. Prepare a pot (one for each seedling you wish to keep) with potting compost as in Step 2. Holding gently onto a true leaf of a seedling, lever it out of the old pot using a pencil to scoop up under the roots. Transfer the seedling to the new pot, using the pencil to make a hole for the roots and then covering them back over with more compost. Place the pots back in a warm light position.

6 Keep checking each plant daily, turning it if necessary to keep the growth upright (it will naturally lean toward the light), and watering when required. Once a plant has outgrown its pot, and if all risk of frost has passed, you can start to harden it off before planting it outside permanently in a large container or the open ground. Harden it off by putting it outside just during the daytime for a few days, then leaving it out at night as well, covered with some horticultural fleece or newspaper for a further couple of days. After that it should be fully acclimatized and so ready for transplanting.

7 When planting out, dig a hole and firm the rootball into the new potting compost or soil, so that there is good contact between the rootball and soil, but do not press down directly around the base of the plant stem because this can break away the young roots. Water each plant thoroughly, and insert a cane or other stake.

8 As the plant grows, use garden twine to tie it to the cane at regular intervals. Once it reaches the top of the cane, pinch out the leading shoot – you should by now have three or four trusses of tomatoes on the plant. Remove the lower leaves as well, as this helps to ripen the fruit, and pinch out any little shoots that appear in the axils of where the trusses or leaves join the main stem.

9 Water each plant whenever needed, and apply a liquid fertilizer (a proprietary tomato feed, or a seaweed-based one) according to the manufacturer's instructions. Wait for your tomatoes to ripen and savour them as soon as possible after picking.

Planting a herb garden

Herbs are excellent plants to cultivate in a mindful garden. They are fragrant, generally have quite small flowers that encourage close inspection, produce a number of different foliage forms that are interesting to touch as well as look at, and they are tasty too. Herbs are easily grown in pots or windowboxes, while allocating some space in the open ground, if you have it, means you can be a bit more creative with their patterns and their varying shapes and textures.

"The man who has planted a garden feels that he has done something for the good of the world."

Charles Dudley Warner,
WRITER

A herb garden with flowering chives (*Allium schoenoprasum*)

Contemplating appreciation

Appreciation is at the very root of mindfulness, because to admire something you first have to notice it is there. How often do you walk past beautiful flowers, or speed through the grocery store checkout barely glancing at the till operator (let alone greeting them), all because you are too wrapped up in your own thoughts? When you are mindful you notice the world around you, and once you have done that you can start to respect it and to understand it. To appreciate something is to see it, to know it and to be thankful for it.

As you plant your herb garden, take a close look at each herb, feel the texture of its foliage and breathe deeply of its fragrance. Treasure your herb garden – for its beauty, its fragrance and for the flavour the herbs bring to your meals. By extension, value the herbs for the pleasure they give to other people when they eat the meals as well.

Carry that sentiment forward and use the herb garden as a reminder to be grateful. Every time you look at the herb garden, think of three things you appreciate. It could be something small (having a cafetière that makes such a delicious cup of coffee) or large (your family, friends or pets). When you value the people in your life, tell them so, and watch the appreciation and happiness spread, whether it be to your family or friends, or to the beleaguered checkout operator.

1 Choose the space for your herb garden. Most herbs prefer full sun, but some (for example, chives/*Allium schoenoprasum*, parsley/*Petroselinum crispum* and lovage/*Levisticum officinale*) will tolerate partial shade. All will need good-quality soil that does not get boggy in winter.

2 Make a list of the herbs you would like to grow. They could be purely culinary, or for a mix of uses such as medicinal and culinary, or just those for scenting the home, perhaps lavender (*Lavandula*) and bergamot (*Monarda didyma*). Check the space required for each type of herb. Roughly, you will be able to fit five herbaceous perennials or small shrubs into a space 1 × 1m (3 × 3ft). Symmetrical and geometric designs work well for herb gardens, often with a low hedge of one herb (chives, thyme/*Thymus* and lavender work well) all the way around the edge, perhaps with larger herbs (e.g. rosemary/*Rosmarinus* or bay/*Laurus nobilis*) marking the corners or centre. Put those you will use most often within easy reach of a path or stepping stones so you do not have to compact the soil to get to them.

3 Water the herbs in their pots well and get your tools ready – a garden fork and rake for preparing the soil, plus a trowel or spade for planting the herbs. Then take a moment to ground yourself (see *Pausing on the threshold*, on pages 55–57).

4 Ensure your soil is free of weeds and large stones, and that you have relieved any compaction by using a garden fork to loosen the soil slightly. Rake the surface level, then lay out the plants. Do not be afraid to spend some time playing about with the design at this stage.

5 Plant your herbs. Dig each hole about twice as wide as each rootball, and to that rootball's depth. Then put in the herbs and firm in the soil around the rootballs. Water the whole area thoroughly, and rake the bare soil to remove any footprints.

6 Once the plants are established, pick a few sprigs. Sit and appreciate your work for a moment, and the scent of the herbs in your fingers. Then take them back to the house to cook with, or put in a vase.

Planting a tree

Planting a tree – especially large ones such as oaks (*Quercus*) – is often described as a selfless act, because by the time the tree reaches its prime we will not be around to enjoy it. Certainly it is a big responsibility: we have to consider the tree's ultimate size, where it will cast shade and so forth, and we must plant it well to ensure the future health and success of the tree. However, we can still gain pleasure from the tree even in its infancy, and from the knowledge that we have done something for the benefit of future generations.

"Even if I knew that tomorrow the world would go to pieces, I would still plant my apple tree."

Martin Luther King, Jr (attributed),

BAPTIST MINISTER AND ACTIVIST

Contemplating patience

Modern life does not engender patience. Technology is geared toward making everything faster; our news is available instantly (often before it is known what is really happening); everybody is in a rush and nice guys finish last. Trees have fortitude. They grow slowly, little by little, and that growth is strong. If they were to develop to their full height in a single year they would be sappy and weak, and would bend and break. If we can adopt the forbearance of trees, we will be able to sustain ourselves over a long period, rather than rushing and burning out. Making changes – learning to be mindful, gardening, working toward a promotion – all take time, and having composure helps us to persevere.

Patience is widely touted to be a virtue, or as something that only saints have, but it is a skill like any other and can be learned. A lack of patience clouds our vision, and not being able to see clearly means we cannot be mindful. Learning to be calm is understanding what makes us impatient: we all have triggers that cause us to be impetuous at first, even indignant or angry, and those emotions do not feel good. We react to situations when we are riled, and need to learn to pause instead.

To increase your chances of being composed rather than upset, consider making changes in your life. If you are overstretched with work and a busy home-life, can you delegate some tasks, or institute some routines for the parts of the day that always need to go roughly the same way (getting the children out of the door to school, for example)? When you become impatient, note what is making you feel that way by taking a step back and a few deep breaths. Do not judge yourself; just notice the trigger, and later you can try to avoid it in future. Separating yourself from the situation might also involve looking at the bigger picture, or trying to see it from the other person's point of view (that lady in front of you in the queue is taking ages to pay and you are in a hurry, but this might be the only time she talks to another person all day). You could even try some exercises to practise being patient, such as deliberately walking (mindfully) home the long way round, or planting seeds the way your toddler wants you to.

Above all visualize your tree – it is still there, slowly growing, being patient. Trees are your link with eternity: think what old trees have seen and what young ones will witness in the years gone and to come. They simply live in each moment, not rushing to get to the next, or wishing away today in anticipation of tomorrow.

1 Gather your tools (a spade and a garden fork), the tree and some garden compost (for mulching). Then take a moment to ground yourself (see *Pausing on the threshold*, on pages 55–57).

2 Water the tree in its pot thoroughly. Use this moment to contemplate the water as it pours into the pot.

3 Dig the hole, 2–3 times as wide as the young tree's roots, and the same depth as its rootball.

4 Fork over the base of the hole to relieve any compaction.

5 Put the tree into the hole and, holding it in place, move the soil back into the hole around the roots. Pour in some water at this stage to ensure it really gets to the roots.

6 Pressing down firmly with your heel, tread around the base of the tree to firm in the soil around the roots, making sure the tree remains upright.

7 Water around the base of the tree thoroughly, then spread some mulch in a thick layer around the base of the tree, making sure that it does not touch the trunk itself.

8 Stand back and admire your work. Is the tree in the right spot? The time to precision plant it is now – even it if means digging it up and moving it ever so slightly. Take another moment to pause for a few more deep breaths before moving on to the next task or tidying up. As you pause, really look at the tree. It may stand on this spot for many hundreds of years, but it is in no rush to get to that point. It will be patient, and so can you be.

Making a terrarium

A terrarium is a world in a jar, an ecosystem in miniature. Aside from being a beautiful miniature garden in its own right, and a great way to bring greenery to a desk or kitchen table, it is ideal for illustrating the interconnections of Nature, both to yourself philosophically (see page 36) and to children as an introduction to certain scientific principles.

"To see a World in a Grain of Sand
And Heaven in a Wild Flower,
Hold Infinity in the palm of your hand
And Eternity in an hour."

William Blake,
POET

Cacti and succulents
require an open terrarium

Contemplating creativity

Being imaginative is not just about being an artist or inventing the latest gadget. Everyone needs creativity every day, at work and at home – to solve the logistics problem in the supply chain, or to find a way to persuade a truculent teenager to tidy their bedroom. Ingenuity can also help you to live life to the full, by enabling you to identify a different way to do something or even a new way to live. However, trying to be creative just does not work. Sitting with a blank piece of paper, telling yourself you will not move until you have come up with the next big thing, will lead only to frustration and stress. On the other hand, you might go to bed and then wake up with an idea so wonderful and simple that you cannot understand how you did not think of it before. This is because, when you were sleeping, the parts of your brain that were inhibiting your creativity were quiet and restful, allowing the imaginative part of your brain to do its work.

Mindfulness works in exactly the same way, but you can do it while being wide awake and get back to your work straight away. It enables you to get some clarity and focus. Your conscious mind is quietened and irrelevant thoughts are not so distracting. Mindfulness meditation has also been shown by a number of studies to boost divergent thinking (the ability of the brain to come up with a range of ideas) and to reduce cognitive rigidity (how past experiences railroad the brain to the same result again and again). In other words, mindfulness can boost your creativity. A quieter mind is more able to see the big idea when it does appear; in a busy mind there is the danger of a good idea getting lost. Some of the big resourceful companies have encouraged mindfulness practice in the workplace, having found it boosts levels of productivity and innovation among its employees.

Practising mindfulness daily, be it a sitting meditation or an active application such as weeding, will in itself help you to be more creative in everyday life. Write down a specific challenge or problem that requires some original ideas or solutions as concisely as possible. Forget all about it and focus completely on making your terrarium, maintaining your attention on the experience of the senses as much as you can. Keep a pad and pen handy: you may find ideas and solutions pop into your head without warning. Write them down and then take your focus back to the terrarium.

1 Choose a vessel in which to create your terrarium – it should be clear glass for maximum light penetration, and you will need to be able to squeeze the plants in through its neck. If the container has a lid, you can create a closed terrarium, in which the air and water are constantly recycled by the plants. However, an open container is also fine – you will just have to water it every now and then.

2 You will also need some activated charcoal pellets to help keep the bacteria down and the water clean. (Pet stores will stock charcoal pellets, because they are the same product as is used for filtering fish tank water.) Other items required are some gravel, sand or glass pebbles and some potting compost (buy this rather than using home-made, because it will have fewer bacteria and soil-borne pathogens that could cause the terrarium plants to rot).

3 Choose your plants. Miniature ferns are ideal, or you could opt for a simple moss base with some twig decorations. Open terrariums could include succulents (closed systems get too humid) as well. You could also add other decorations, provided they are of a material that will not rot or rust.

4 Take a moment to ground yourself (see *Pausing on the threshold*, on pages 55–57). Put a layer of gravel, then one of charcoal, then one of compost into the container. The compost layer needs to be deep enough to accommodate the rootballs, and the three layers together should reach to about one-third the height of the container. Using a funnel helps keep the layers neat.

5 Plant your plants firmly into the compost layer. (You can wash off the soil and tease out the roots before planting to make them smaller and the planting easier.)

6 Cover any bare compost with more gravel or moss, then water the plants very slowly to soak the compost, but no more. Seal the terrarium with the lid if it has one.

7 Put your terrarium in bright, but not direct, sunlight (direct light will heat the interior of the container to intolerable levels for the plants). You may need to rotate the container regularly for even growth of the plants within.

8 Other than cleaning the glass and trimming back plants that are growing too large, closed terrariums are maintenance-free. Open terrariums will need their glass cleaning too, but also the occasional watering.

A potted gift

When we care about others and want to give them something, we experience a feeling of abundance. Gardening is a joy, and passing that on to others in the form of a gift of a potted plant is a generous act. If the recipient is already a keen gardener, then they will cherish it for being a beautiful addition to their garden. If they have yet to try gardening, they will appreciate it for the opportunity to try something new and stimulate their curiosity. Gifts are also treasured all the more for being home-made, because they show the time and effort that has gone into creating them.

"The lesson I have thoroughly learnt, and wish to pass on to others, is to know the enduring happiness that the love of a garden gives."

Gertrude Jekyll,
GARDEN DESIGNER AND AUTHOR

Growing crocus in pots allows you to appreciate their beauty and fragrance at close hand.

Contemplating generosity

Largesse is not about buying lavish presents at Christmas, or giving away all your money. We know that material possessions do not make us truly happy. Far better is to offer our time and energy, and to give thanks, praise and encouragement. These things mean much more to the recipient. The gift that bestows the most is attention. To truly listen to a friend when they are talking, or to our spouse when they tell us about their day, is the generosity that counts. Practising mindfulness helps us to clear our minds and bring focus to the times when it really matters, so that we can be bountiful with our attention. The more practised we become, the easier it will be to extend this philanthropy beyond our immediate circle to others – strangers such as till clerks.

However, giving yourself all the time is not a route to contentment, because it will lead to eventual burnout. We have to have something to give, and to that end we must also be generous to ourselves, nurture ourselves and allow our bodies and minds a chance to rest and relax, as well as enjoy ourselves. As with all things, it is a question of balance. On the reverse, when you resist giving – your attention, time or something else – ask yourself why. Is it because you are annoyed at the interruption, and you think what you are doing is more important? There is a story of a Buddhist monk who had founded a school in Tibet. He was in the middle of leading a long ceremony when a child wandered in and asked for help with his homework. Many of us would have dismissed the child and his request as being less important than the completion of the ceremony, but the monk did not. He stopped what he was doing, sat down with the child until the homework was done, then completed his ceremony (for the waiting congregation). To the monk, the child was as worthy of his attention as his own task and he gave it freely and without grudge.

Plants too can teach us this lesson – they offer us their beauty, their food and their shelter without hope of return, and so this project is noble in three ways. The plants we use are generous to us as we make the present. We are also being kind to ourselves in spending some time working with plants

– the garden nurtures us as we nurture the garden – and we are, of course, being bountiful in then passing on the pot that we put our time and effort into making. As we give it away we can hope that the recipient will get as much happiness out of the plants as we have, and potentially a new-found interest in gardening that will also bring them joy.

1 Collect together your materials and plants. Use a terracotta pot or similar planter, some potting compost and sufficient plants to fit the container. The pot should look full, but the plants still need space to breathe. For this potted gift you could use plants that you have divided from your own borders, or grown from seed or cuttings, or else buy a selection from a garden centre or nursery. Think about whom you are giving the pot to and what they like – would they appreciate certain colours or plants over others? Would they prefer edible or ornamental plants? Think about the plants too: if they are going to be in the pot together, they all need to have similar requirements: for example, do not put a bog plant in with one that prefers dry conditions. Then take a moment to ground yourself (see *Pausing on the threshold*, on pages 55–57).

2 Fill the bottom of the pot with potting compost, and tap it down to ensure there are no large air pockets. Put in the plants, shifting them around to best effect. If any plants are particularly rootbound, tease out the roots slightly before planting them.

3 Fill in around the sides of the rootballs with more compost, firming them all in properly so there is good contact between the roots and the new compost. Once all the gaps between the rootballs have been filled in, ensure there is at least 1cm (½in) between the top of the compost and the rim of the pot.

4 Water the pot thoroughly and then let it sit for a while. This may expose gaps, so fill in any with more compost and add some at the top if the level has sunk.

5 To make the surface of the compost more attractive, you could cover it with a layer of moss. Sphagnum moss is available to buy from garden centres and florists, but you could rake some out of your lawn instead, give it a wash to remove any bugs, then dress thickly around the base of the plants so that the compost is covered.

6 You could also add decorative touches – for example, a pot of spring bulbs could be enhanced by the addition of a few sprigs of pussy willow (*Salix* species) or corkscrew hazel (*Corylus avellana* 'Contorta'). These are available from florists if you do not have anything like that in the garden or you are unable to forage any. Some handwritten labels with the plant names would be a nice touch, too, that gardeners both old and new would appreciate.

"The important thing is not to stop questioning. Curiosity has its own reason for existing."

Albert Einstein,
THEORETICAL PHYSICIST

Planting a flower clock

A flower clock was an idea first put forward by the 18th-century botanist Carl Linnaeus, the man responsible for the binomial botanical Latin plant naming system still used today. His concept was simple and not dissimilar to a sundial, because he had observed that certain flowers opened at specific times of day. He therefore proposed that, by planting these flowers in a clock formation, visitors to the clock could tell what time of day it was, by seeing which flowers were open. The botanical reality was not quite so simple of course (time zones, day length and the plants themselves were all far too variable), and it was an idea that never really took off. However, the fact that the idea "horologium florae" still persists is evidence of the irresistibility of the concept.

Because most of the plants Linnaeus identified were wild flowers that would most certainly be classed as weeds in today's gardens, the flower clock project here collects together a few plants that change over the course of the day, even though they will not be able to tell us the actual time. The aim is to plant up a pot that appears different – if looked at closely enough – each time we glance at it.

This obviously encourages the skill of mindful observation, but it should also stimulate curiosity. How does a flower bud track the sun across the sky through the day? What makes a flower open and close? How does it do it? Why? The answers to all of these questions can be found in basic horticultural textbooks, or online (see *Further resources*, on pages 218–19), and hopefully you will be interested enough to seek them out.

California poppies
(*Eschscholzia californica*)

Contemplating curiosity

If you are inquisitive, you are looking around you with a sense of wonder, searching for something that you have not seen before or seeking an explanation as to why something is. You are using your senses and are focused on them intently. In other words, you are being mindful. Curiosity and mindfulness go hand in hand: mindfulness feeds curiosity and curiosity feeds mindfulness.

Viewing life with wonder, with a "beginner's mind", is one of the fastest ways to forge new connections between neurons in your mind. The tired contemptuous pathways of experience are those that create habit and autopilot; curiosity helps us to experience life fully. Even if it is something you do all the time, try looking at your surroundings with fresh eyes, listening with fresh ears. For example, when making a cup of tea look, listen and feel the process as if you have never seen, heard or felt it before. When it comes to drinking the tea, savour it as if it were your first ever. You will not be able to override your experiences completely – and nor would you want to, because they provide invaluable information (do not pour the boiling water over your hand, it will hurt) and insight – so they will apply filters to all your actions. However, try whenever possible to gaze with fresh rather than tired eyes. For example, when you next see your spouse or a close friend, are you really studying their face, or just seeing what you think you know they look like (re-cognition)?

Curiosity reveals the richness of the world, and the natural world, and shows you how little you actually know. By being inquisitive you strengthen your mind, suspend judgment and open yourself up to possibilities. Be probing also about how your mind and body work. Do you feel physically different when you are anxious? What happens if you take a few deep breaths if you are angry? Be curious about your experience as well as about the world.

1 Collect together a large container, some potting compost, a trowel, and some of the plants from the list (see *Flower clock plants*, on page 201). If you are including the morning glory (*Ipomoea*) you will also need three tall canes or other narrow stakes and some garden twine. Then take a moment to ground yourself (see *Pausing on the threshold*, on pages 55–57).

2 Fill the base of the container with compost. Then arrange the plants (while still in their pots) on the compost and check that their height will be correct when finally planted. Top up the compost beneath them if required.

3 Remove each plant from its pot and insert into the container. Add the canes if needed, tying them together at the top into a tripod.

4 Fill in around the plants with more compost so they are all firmly embedded in the container. You should leave a small gap under the rim so that the container does not overflow when watered.

5 Water the container thoroughly. If the compost level sinks after this, just add a bit more on top.

Flower clock plants

These plants all open either only in the sun or only at dusk, or they bloom for only a single day, or are only fragrant at certain times of day. The flower buds (but not the mature flower) of one will even track the movement of the sun through the day. It is up to you to be curious and find out which does what. The information here for each plant is to help you plan an attractive container suitable for your garden. Take care not to plant out half-hardy plants until all risk of frost has passed. It would be best to acquire the annuals as young plants, but if you prefer to sow seeds, follow the instructions for *Growing tomatoes from seed* (see pages 176–79) and refer to the seed packet for further information.

Left to right: *Gladiolus tristis* var. *concolor* (evening flower); *Tagetes patula* (French marigold); *Hemerocallis* (daylily); *Nicotiana alata* 'Grandiflora' (flowering tobacco); *Gazania* (treasure flower)

Crocus (spring or autumn bulb, to 10cm/4in high; white/orange/purple)

Calendula officinalis (pot marigold; summer half-hardy annual, to 30cm/12in high; orange)

Eschscholzia californica (California poppy; summer annual, to 30cm/12in high; red/orange/yellow)

Gazania (treasure flower; summer half-hardy perennial, to 30cm/12in high; many colours)

Gladiolus tristis (evening flower; summer half-hardy to hardy bulb, to 40cm/16in high; white/cream)

Helianthus annuus (sunflower; summer half-hardy annual, to several metres in height depending on cv; yellow/red/cream)

Hemerocallis (daylily; summer hardy perennial, to 1–2m/3–6½ft high; many colours)

Ipomoea alba (belle de nuit), *I. indica* (blue dawn flower; summer half-hardy annual climbers, to 6m/20ft high; purple/white)

Nicotiana alata (flowering tobacco; summer half-hardy annual, to 2m/6½ft high; white)

"The highest reward for a person's toil is not what they get for it, but what they become by it."

John Ruskin,

ART CRITIC, SOCIAL THINKER AND PHILANTHROPIST

Creating a mandala

"Mandala" is a Sanskrit word that loosely translates as "circle", yet it has a far deeper meaning than that. It is used in both Hindu and Buddhist religions, and the concept is also found in some Christian history and in the traditions of the Navajo Indians in North America. In essence, the mandala is a symbol for the entire cosmos, for all life on earth and beyond, for the life forces that we can see and those we cannot. It is a reminder of the infinite and of life's interconnections.

Mandalas can be made following a pre-made blueprint or to a personal design, and can be incredibly intricate or as simple as the yin-yang symbol. They can be large or small. In Tibet the creation of mandalas is still used as a means of spiritual practice. Highly sophisticated perfect designs are made using different colours of sand or crushed glass, a process sometimes taking several hours or even days. Once finished, the whole design is swept away. The object is not to create a permanent structure or something that can be kept, but to use the making of the mandala as a meditative process, and the relinquishment of it as a lesson in impermanence. It can be difficult to see something that has taken so much time and effort to create being destroyed in a matter of moments, but learning to come to terms with that is part of each monk's journey to enlightenment.

Here, the aim is something similar. Create a mandala in your garden, all the while knowing it is an impermanent and transient installation, and use the time while you are making it as a chance to take a break from the pressures of everyday life. Such regrouping is a form of being kind to yourself, and you cannot be considerate to others if you are not first gentle with yourself.

Contemplating impermanence

Change is inevitable. Trying to hold onto the idea of everything lasting forever, like a fairy-tale ending, is like trying to retain a breath in the body – it just does not work, and actually prevents us from enjoying the present. In fact simply noticing the breath as it moves in and out of our lungs is an acknowledgment of impermanence in itself. Practising mindfulness teaches us to realize that nothing lasts forever – good times or bad times – and also gives us the ability to appreciate each moment. We can accept, or even embrace, impermanence.

When we know that something will not last, we enjoy it all the more for what it is. Saying goodbye to someone or something is sad, but if we are mindful we can take comfort in knowing that we did not waste our time together and we truly appreciated what we had. Accepting impermanence can bring clarity to our lives. It helps us to understand that everyone is growing and changing, and therefore perhaps a little compassion and forgiveness would not go amiss. It also assists us in realizing what is really important, right now, in that moment.

1 Choose a design for your mandala. Many images are available on the internet. Some of the adult colouring books (especially those geared for mindfulness) have mandala designs, or you can create your own. Take into account how much time you are going to dedicate to its creation – half an hour, or an afternoon?

2 Choose the materials. Gather these from your garden or forage some from a local park. You could use a wide range of natural materials, and they need not all be the same in a single mandala. You could opt for soil (wet and dry will give two different colours), sand, stones and gravel, grass clippings, flowers and/or petals, leaves, twigs, fruit and vegetables, pine cones or seeds. Try designing mandalas from different materials depending on the season: for example, autumn leaves and summer petals. You could even draw a mandala in the snow.

3 You will need a flat surface on which to create the mandala, such as patio or lawn. If you have neither, choose a large board or table. Then take a moment to ground yourself (see *Pausing on the threshold*, on pages 55–57).

4 Lay out your materials in your desired pattern. As you work, try to keep the focus on what you are doing, and enjoy the time simply to spend with yourself, being creative.

5 Once you have finished, either sweep away the mandala at once, or leave it to be slowly destroyed by the elements. Either way, remember that the point was the process, not the end-result.

Cutting a posy

Everybody likes to receive a gift of flowers, and a seasonal posy from your own garden is so much more personal than a store-bought bouquet of imported blooms. There is no need to give the posy away of course – keep it for yourself to take to work (a reminder of the garden on your desk at all times) or put it on your bedside table. The posy will remind you that you have plenty to be grateful for, especially in the garden – a source of such beautiful, perhaps fragrant flowers.

Growing flowers for cutting is a lovely use of part of your garden, and many straightforward-to-grow annual plants are perfect for cutting. However, if you do not have the space, it is just as easy to put together a posy of other types of flowering plants and their foliage from the garden.

"From heavy hearts and doleful dumps, the garden chaseth quite."

Anon,
16TH-CENTURY POET

Snapdragons (*Antirrhinum majus*)
and sweet peas (*Lathyrus odoratus*)
are both good flowers for cutting.

Posy plants

Almost any flowers can be used for cutting, but some good ones to grow for small posies include the following. Many herbs make good filler/foliage plants as well.

Alchemilla mollis (lady's mantle)

Allium (ornamental onion)

Ammi majus (bullwort)

Astrantia major (greater masterwort)

Briza maxima (greater quaking grass)

Centaurea cyanus (cornflower)

Cosmos bipinnatus (cosmea)

Dahlia

Helenium (sneezeweed)

Lathyrus odoratus (sweet pea)

Lunaria annua (honesty)

Muscari (grape hyacinth)

Narcissus (daffodil)

Nigella damascena (love-in-a-mist)

Panicum 'Frosted Explosion' (crab grass)

Papaver somniferum (opium poppy)

Rosa (rose)

Rudbeckia hirta (black-eyed Susan)

Scabiosa atropurpurea (sweet scabious)

Tulipa (tulips)

Visnaga daucoides

Contemplating kindness

There is more to mindfulness than pure, dry observation. Bringing kindness and compassion into your practice is not just about lots of hugging and warm fuzzy feelings. Many scientific studies have shown that it significantly enhances not only the efficacy of the mindfulness practice itself, but also general wellbeing and health – both emotional and physical. These studies have demonstrated that "loving-kindness" meditation has an immediate short-term effect, as well as a long-term impact, and has many advantages over mindfulness practice with no emotional overtones.

Mindfulness without thoughtfulness can be cold, even boring, because it is using only your head. By introducing the heart as well, and looking at the world with compassion and even love, you bring kindness to your day-to-day experience. Mindfulness benefits your amenability because otherwise how can you be aware of who needs such gentleness? Likewise, how can you know whether you are being considerate, or the opposite, if you are not aware? Introducing kindness helps you be empathetic toward your fellow human beings and spreads goodwill and warmth in your social interactions.

If you feel generally happy and relaxed after a mindfulness practice, then the chances are that you are already being loving and compassionate. If you cannot wait for it to be over, then perhaps you are not. Kindness is not just applicable to other people; it is also essential to be generous to yourself, particularly during mindfulness practice. If you are going to accept your thoughts and feelings just as they are, you must view them with benevolence, because being self-critical will only make it worse. Look on your mindfulness practice as like teaching a child to walk – it is that basic. Gentle encouragement is the order of the day; harsh reproaches will not help. If unpleasant thoughts and feelings arise during your practice, simply notice them for what they are without any sort of judgment and return the

focus to the senses. Take it easy on yourself and smile – mindfulness should be an enjoyable process.

No matter whom the recipient, as you cut flowers and foliage for a posy be grateful for the chance to get out in the fresh air, for the plants in your garden and for the supply of beautiful flowers that you can take into the home. If you are keeping the posy for yourself, when you look at it, use it as a reminder to appreciate the garden and these lovely flowers. If your kind gesture is to give it away, be thankful for the friend or family to whom you are donating it, and that you are able to spread a little happiness.

1 Gather up your secateurs (hand pruners) or a pair of sharp scissors and head out into the garden, *Pausing on the threshold* (see pages 55–57) for a moment or two.

2 You do not need a lot of blooms – a posy is intended to be small – or indeed to have any flowers at all in it. A collection of different shapes, textures and shades of foliage can be just as attractive, especially during winter. Do not forget that stems and berries can add interest too. As a rule you want to be able to hold the posy easily in your hand once it is tied.

3 Cut the flowers and/or foliage, giving yourself plenty of stem to work with, while also taking care to make the incision just above a bud so that each plant will regrow tidily. Take the posy material to a worktop and strip off the lower leaves.

4 Then hold the centrepiece flower in your hand – a tall spike or single spectacular bloom – while arranging the other blooms and/or foliage around it, putting the other stems slightly lower in each ring around the central one so they all have plenty of space.

5 Once you have arranged the flowers and/or foliage to your satisfaction, use a piece of garden twine to wind round the stems a few times, then tie it off. You could add some ribbon over the twine if you wanted.

6 Neaten the stems by cutting them all to the same length, then place the posy in some water until you need it (or just put it in a vase for yourself immediately).

Collecting seeds

There is much to be grateful for in a garden in autumn. The flowers that were once so bright have faded and withered, and the leaves are turning to brown. Yet among the faded flowers and dry leaves are the hidden treasures of seeds and fruits, which give hope for the seasons ahead and delicious bounty for the here and now. The fruits and seeds are never wasted. If we do not collect them, animals will, or they will fall to the ground and rot, returning their nutrients to the soil (or we will return them via the compost heap), or maybe they will lie in the soil and germinate next season. As we collect seeds, we accept that the season has changed, and it is time to enjoy the autumn.

Save seeds from the garden to eat – for example, coriander/cilantro (*Coriandrum sativum)*, fennel (*Foeniculum*), dill (*Anethum graveolens*) and poppies (*Papaver*) – or to grow next year. The latter can be a fun exercise because the seeds will not necessarily come true to the original plant, especially if they were from a hybrid, whose seedlings may possess a variety of flower colours or other differences. The seeds could be enclosed within fruit or vegetables, or berries, or they may be dry on the plant. The instructions on the following pages outline the general principles when collecting dry seeds and seedheads. For sources of more information, see *Further resources*, on pages 218–19.

Contemplating gratitude

Mindfulness and gratitude are strongly linked in a positive feedback loop, or virtuous circle. Without mindfulness we cannot spot all the things that are going well in our lives. The more we identify, the more we are thankful for, and the more we are grateful, the more we notice for which we should be appreciative! Gratitude is a skill just like riding a bike – it takes practice and perseverance, but with time we can develop what many mindfulness teachers call the "gratitude attitude".

The brain has a natural bias toward negativity and, if we do not regularly take note of all the things that make us happy, we forget about them and fall back into the "doleful dumps" again. Incorporating some appreciation into our daily routines, and some mindfulness to help us identify things, can have a massive effect on personal health and wellbeing. One study showed as much as a 25 percent increase in happiness and health. The more we notice and are grateful, the more those neurons fire together and wire together more strongly.

It is possible simply to sit and think of things that you are thankful for, but the studies show that writing them down has an even greater effect. Keeping a "gratitude journal" – a little notebook in which you jot down three or five things for which you are appreciative every day – is a simple way to include gratitude in your life. If there is some part of your life that it seems impossible to be grateful for, try turning it on its head. For example, a long commute could be a real trial, but instead you could relish the time in which you can read a book, because you would not otherwise have space in your day to indulge your love of reading.

As you go about the garden collecting seeds, appreciate the task for what it is, and be grateful for the plants bounty and for the chance to get out in the fresh air, for the plants in your garden and for the supply of beautiful fruits.

1 Source some paper bags or envelopes and garden twine, plus a pen for labelling your bags.

2 Collect seed on a dry day. As you are about to venture outdoors, take a moment to ground yourself (see *Pausing on the threshold*, on pages 55–57). You need the seeds to be mature; that is the point at which the plant would shed them. If you are not confident about judging this timing, you can tie a paper bag over the seedhead(s), fixing it securely to the stem below, so that as the seeds begin to drop they will be caught in the bag beneath. You can then cut the stem and hang it upside down until the rest of the seeds dry and fall, or can be shaken, out of the seedhead.

3 With plants such as poppies (*Papaver*), the seeds are ready when they can be shaken around audibly in the seedhead and the little apertures below the top rim are open. The seeds of umbelliferous plants such as fennel (*Foeniculum*) and dill (*Anethum graveolens*) will be dry, brown and easily dislodged from the plant.

4 Shake or scrape the seeds into your paper bag or envelope, either directly off the plant or by cutting the seedhead off and shaking them out at a table. Try to place just the seeds and as little "chaff" as possible in the bag/envelope.

5 Seal the bag/envelope so the seeds cannot escape and label it with the plant's name and the date on which you collected the seeds.

6 Store seeds in an airtight container in a cool dry environment, until you are ready to sow them.

Shed reminder sheet

There is no wrong way to practise mindfulness. The more you do it, the easier it becomes, but it will take practice and perseverance. As little as 10 minutes' mindfulness in the garden every day will have huge benefits to your health and wellbeing.

Being mindful

 Mindfulness is a moment-by-moment awareness of the sensations of your body, your feelings, your thoughts and the world around you. Your attention may move from one thing to another, yet you are constantly aware.

 Be curious. Approach the world with a beginner's mind or a childlike wonder.

 Be kind in your mindfulness, to yourself and to others.

 Appreciate the world around you and the interconnections within it.

 Be grateful for all that you have – all the more for knowing its impermanence.

Starting

 Take some deep breaths, in through the nose and out through the mouth.

 Feel the body relax and the weight of your body on your feet.

 Become aware of your body and how it feels today. Do not judge, just observe.

Mindful gardening

 While being conscious of your body, choose a rhythmic movement such as walking and focus the attention on that.

 Awareness of the garden around you will follow.

 When you look, listen, touch, smell and taste the garden, fully experience it through your senses and avoid narrating what you are doing.

 If your thoughts get carried away, use the senses as an anchor to bring the attention back to what you are doing and then to the rhythmic movement.

 Do this without judgment or self-criticism.

 Finish the exercise with a conscious stop in a period of awareness, rather than allowing the attention to drift away and not getting it back.

 Once you have finished, draw a line under the exercise, and do not analyse your performance.

"People usually consider walking on water or in thin air a miracle. But I think the real miracle is… to walk on earth."

Thich Nhat Hanh,
MONK AND PEACE ACTIVIST

Further resources

MINDFULNESS

This book covers the basics of secular mindfulness, but there is much more to learn and discover. A good place to start is the Headspace app (www.headspace.com/), which has guided audio meditations for many aspects of life and the mind, as well as guided applications of mindfulness for everyday tasks such as cooking and running.

For more information on mindfulness, look also at:
www.oxfordmindfulness.org/, the website of the Oxford Mindfulness Centre, a department of the University of Oxford, a world leader in research into mindfulness.

www.mindful.org/, a website and magazine dedicated to all things to do with mindfulness.

GARDENING

The website of the Royal Horticultural Society (RHS), www.rhs.org.uk/, offers a wealth of information and advice on everything from plant selection to wildlife gardening (especially the Plants for Pollinators scheme) and from practical gardening skills to pond design and saving seed.

Local wildlife trusts (www.wildlifetrusts.org/) also have information on gardening for wildlife.

Other invaluable books include the following:

A Little History of British Gardening (Jenny Uglow, 2005) is an entertaining and informative look at the development of gardens as places of leisure.

Second Nature: A Gardener's Education (Michael Pollan, 1991) details the author's creation of a new garden and his relationship with Nature along the way.

RHS Latin for Gardeners (Lorraine Harrison, 2012) explains the etymology of plant names.

While *The Language of Flowers* (Vanessa Diffenbaugh, 2011) is a novel, it nonetheless contains much good information about the meanings of different flowers.

Creating a Forest Garden (Martin Crawford, 2010) is the definitive work on incorporating edible plants into all levels of a garden.

Food for Free (Richard Mabey, 1972, new edition 2012) is an excellent guide to identifying edible plants, including wild flowers and weeds.

Botany for Gardeners (Brian Capon, third edition 2010), *RHS Science and the Garden* (D S Ingram *et al.*, 2008) and *RHS Botany for Gardeners: The Art and Science of Gardening Explained & Explored* (Geoff Hodge, 2013) are all good introductions to horticultural science.

Index

Acknowledgements

'This is a book that I thought should be written, and so I am very grateful to Alison Starling and Rae Spencer-Jones for giving me the opportunity to do so. Writing the text is, however, just the beginning and I'd also like to thank Polly Poulter, Juliette Norsworthy and all the team at Octopus for transforming those bare words into these lovely pages. At home, it inevitably fell to my wonderful husband to keep things running while I worked into the night, so thank you Kevin (as always) for your support and encouragement.'

Picture Credits